ST. PHILIP'S ANGLICAN CHURCH
2855 LACON STREET
REGINA, SK
S4N 2A9

54

ST. PHILIP'S ANGLICAN CHURCH
2855 LACON STREET
REGINA, SK
S4N 2A9

Rooted in God

Parables from the Garden by
Marcia Hollis

with illustrations by
Saskia Walther

an expanded and illustrated edition of Down to Earth: Thoughts on God and Gardening

Anglican Book Centre
Toronto, Canada

1983
Anglican Book Centre
600 Jarvis Street
Toronto, Ontario
Canada M4Y 2J6

Cover design by Saskia Walther

Typesetting by Jay Tee Graphics Ltd.

Printed in Canada

Canadian Cataloguing in Publication Data

Hollis, Marcia
  Rooted in God: parables from the garden

ISBN 0-919891-05-5

1. Christian life - 1960 - 2. Parables.
I. Title.

BV 4501.2.H64 1983   248.4   C83-098812-2

to Reg
whose roots
run deep

Contents

Down to Earth

The joy of making mud pies is one of my earliest childhood memories. I remember the ooze of the mud as we picked it up by globby handfuls and patted it into pans and set it out to bake in the hot sun. And I remember the mud in the springtime when we were told not to step on the grass but we did anyway (just on the edges) because of the lovely squishy feeling when our boots sank in the mud.

All of a sudden, you get too old for this. You walk on the sidewalk and you keep your hands clean and you look with great disdain at little children playing in the mud. Mud is no longer fun. It's dirt and drudgery — the enemy of clean floors and polished shoes. Oh, it's a terrible thing to grow up.

I was all grown up and married, with three children, before I rediscovered that half-forgotten childhood pleasure. We moved from an apartment to a house with a garden — at least, "garden" is one way of describing it. Actually it was a new house on the edge of town, and the garden was a fairly square plot covered with yellow-green grass. We lived there for a year before we tried to do much with it.

An observable law in community living is that good gardeners normally have an improving effect on their neighbours. And all of our neighbours, in the slightly older houses up the street, were very good gardeners. Their lawns were immaculate, their hedges were clipped and tidy, and their flower beds were ablaze with bloom from May to October.

The contrast with our own sparse herbiage was too much. With the best of intentions, but little knowledge, I prepared to do battle with poor drainage, outcrops of the Laurentian Shield (we live on it!), mysterious blights and fungi, and an inexplicable assortment of poison-proof bugs.

Now I'm not much of a gardener. My thumbs (all ten of them) tend to be more black than green, and I've never been able to keep a house plant much longer than three months. I really only got out in that garden from a dire kind of necessity to keep the family head up. I was just going to stick in a few petunias, and maybe a maple tree if ambition lasted that long.

But to plant, you have to dig. And in digging, you get muddy. There was mud on my shoes and my face and my hands, and I thought what a mess it was and what a chore it would be to get all cleaned up. Somewhere a memory stirred. My foot sank into the mud around the newly planted tree and I remembered the innocent joy of getting dirty.

How many chances do adults have to reclaim the pleasures of childhood? For the rest of the summer and the next and the next, I dug and planted to my heart's content. Bushes, plants, flowers, shrubs, trees, anything that would grow! Some things survived; others didn't. I got books from the library and asked the neighbors. In the ensuing welter of failures and small successes, I was bound to learn something about basic gardening. Much more to my surprise, I learned something about God.

Jesus told us to consider the lilies (Matt 6:28) if we wanted to know something about God's care and concern for us. I never had much success with lilies, but I think the same principle applies in the rest of the garden. When we talk about God or our prayer life or any spiritual thing, the subject is so intangible to our understanding that we must of necessity explain by comparisons. There is no other way. How often Jesus said: "The kingdom of heaven is *like* . . ."

About the time that I first began to run into "dry" periods in prayer, I also learned what effect dryness has on plants and how they benefit from it. It helped to think about this, and gradually other gardening analogies came to mind. One can't claim originality for this kind of thing. I think God teaches us through the things around us, if our minds are even half-turned towards him. And nature is one of the most effective instruments of his teaching, even in this age of cement-block apartment houses and asphalt paving. Similar thoughts are equally reflected in the Bible, and by Christians of many persuasions through the ages.

A garden is a lovesome thing, God wot!
Rose plot,
Fringed pool,
Fern'd grot —
The veriest school
Of peace; and yet the fool
Contends that God is not —
Not God! in gardens! when the eve is cool?
Nay, but I have a sign;
'Tis very sure God walks in mine.

Thomas Edward Brown

My Friends, that are gone, and are going, over to Plant, and make outward Plantations in America, Keep your own Plantations in your hearts, with the Spirit and Power of God, that your own Vines and Lilies be not hurt.

George Fox

The Ground

In a now-familiar phrase, Paul Tillich has described God as *the ground of our being*. And St Paul wrote long before: "In him we live and move and have our being" (Acts 17:28). God is the ground of our being, and we in a sense are like plants in this ground, living as separate entities but as closely connected to him as a plant is to the earth and not able to exist otherwise.

The relationship of plants to their soil is much more involved than the average city-dweller realizes, although modern farmers certainly know all about it. Agricultural science can analyze soil content these days and say what plants will thrive in it. The land that grows good wheat is not especially suited to asparagus.

Sometimes window-box and other small-scale gardeners get into the way of thinking that "good black earth" is the only earth worth having, and that you can't grow anything really worthwhile without a rich soil. It depends on what you are trying to grow. The whole world is covered with green and growing plant life. But it isn't all petunias! Some plants can't take the rich soil. They go crazy in it, put out nothing but leaves, and forget to produce flowers and seed.

We have a rock garden in front of the house which was more or less thrown together after the builders left. In our area it is one of two possible solutions to a banked hill in front of the steps, and our next-door neighbours have one too. Partly through laziness and partly because we just didn't know any better, we bought an assortment of rock-garden plants and tucked them into the gravelly dirt that the builders had dumped and bulldozed into place.

"You'll never grow anything in that junk!" warned the neighbours. Painstakingly, they cleaned out the pebbles and worked a load of rich black soil into what was left. The result, sad to say, was that our rock garden thrived and theirs didn't. It was the only time our gardening inexperience paid off! It seems that rock-garden plants do better in a poor soil resembling their native alpine conditions. Our neighbours ended up putting in comfort-loving pansies and petunias.

Some people seem to expect God to be like rich black earth. They go around talking about their experience of him, his ever-abiding presence with them, his great goodness to them, and other signs and tokens of his love. It may never be said in so many words, but the implication is strong that if you don't have all this, then you haven't got anything and you better keep looking. An attitude like this leaves a good many Christians in something of a bind, for it would be equally futile either to deny the reality of the other person's experience of God or yet to pretend that one had had the same experience oneself. An experience of God cannot be manufactured.

God is not rich black earth! And to maintain this kind of attitude is to put him on a level with those plastic bags of homogenized, pasteurized, fertilized, and guaranteed black stuff they sell for growing house plants. God abides unmoved, but within himself. He is full of infinite variety and change. He is a creator, not a factory, and each of his creatures is an individual with personal needs and desires.

Only God can meet our deepest need, but he does it on his terms. He knows what we need and when we need and how much we need. And if you happen to be a spiritual petunia, you'll get rich, black earth. But if you're a spiritual cactus (and their bloom in the desert is a beautiful sight to behold), you won't get anything but dry sand.

And thus I saw full surely that it is readier to us to come to the knowing of God than to know our own soul. For our soul is so deep-grounded in God, and so endlessly treasured, that we may not come to the knowing thereof till we have first knowing of God, which is the Maker, to whom it is oned. . . . God is nearer to us than our own soul: for he is the Ground in whom our soul standeth, and he is the mean that keepeth the substance and the sense-nature together so that they shall never dispart. For our soul sitteth in God in very rest, and our soul standeth in God in very strength, and our soul is kindly rooted in God in endless love.

Julian of Norwich

Man without God is a seed upon the wind: driven this way and that, and finding no place of lodgement and germination.

T.S. Eliot

Roots

A good root system is the most important part of a plant. Nothing can survive for long without adequate roots, for though they are hidden and unseen, they support both the weight and the needs of the branches and leaves above them. A tree or shrub with a good root system may be broken or cut back almost to the earth and still be able to regenerate itself. But similar damage to the root system will kill the tree.

Writing to the Ephesians, St Paul prayed that they might have their roots and foundations in love (Eph 3:17). And by this, he meant the love of God. We should be *rooted* in God, who is the *ground* of our being.

A plant has two parts: the stalks and flowers and leaves which distinguish it and are attractive to look at, and then the roots, which are not seen but which play such a vital part in the whole life of the plant. So have we two parts: that which is seen and heard, our physical form, our words and actions, and then that which is not seen, our thoughts and feelings, our soul.

Jesus said we should not worry about those who can destroy the body, but should fear God who has power to destroy the soul (Luke 12:4–5). Our soul is our root in God. The root of the plant is its hold on life. As a plant can grow again after total destruction of its seen part, so we too can hope for life after death if our roots are deep in the love of God. Those who destroy the life of the body do not touch the essential roots, but if they destroy the soul, then they are destroying the roots. No plant can survive that.

Roots have essentially two purposes in the life of the plant. The first is to nourish it; the second is to hold it up. Roots get nourishment from the soil both from the minerals that are in the ground and also from the water which it contains. Jesus said that we should ask God for "living water" (John 4:10). Our root in the love of God needs this living water, and we receive it by our belief in Jesus (John 7:37-39).

Sometimes we go through what are technically known as "dry periods," when the love of God seems very remote and hardly to be believed. We pray, if we pray at all, in a kind of despair because we have no sense of his promised nearness, no joy, and little faith. This is not the time to give up!

Plants have their seasons of dryness too, and with good reason. Roots form where they can most easily find water. If it rains constantly, or if you are faithful with the hose and sprinkler, your grass and flowers will be green and lush. But a sudden dry season (always, always when you are away on holiday) will leave them utterly stranded. With roots only near the surface where they were accustomed to find water, they will certainly wither and die. It is important for every plant to grow deep roots in order to weather the dry seasons. And by the same token, it is only through the dry seasons that a plant extends its roots and pushes them down into the earth in a search for water.

The bigger plants, the trees and shrubs, have what is called a tap root — a big, heavy, thick root that doesn't fool around but goes almost straight down into the earth before sending out little tendrils of water-gathering rootlets. The tree puts out other small roots close to the surface as well to catch rainfall, but these are less important. In transplanting such a tree, it is the tap root which may not be broken.

In a drought it is the small plants that suffer first — the annuals because their roots are shallow, and the grass for the same reason. But the big trees with all their foliage to support do not show the heat for a long time, and are able to give merciful shade instead. Their roots are deep in the earth, deep where the water wells up.

Our own "dry periods" are sent for the same reason that the plants in my garden suffer dryness — so that we may be rooted more deeply. The plants have to push their roots; they have to look for water. We must do the same thing. Jesus told us to ask and seek and knock (Matt 7:7). There is no doubt about the finding, but we must make the effort.

The second function of roots, after feeding the plant, is to hold it up. A newly planted bush or tree almost always needs some extra support until its roots are growing firmly in the ground. Otherwise a stiff wind will come along and blow it over. It is the roots that hold a tree steady.

Trees that grow up sheltered from the wind, as in a clump of trees, grow tall and thin, and their roots are often shallow. When one such tree is singled out and left standing while the others are cut down to leave room for houses and roads and parks, it is left without the protection it depended on. It is not unusual for such a tree to be blown over in the first big storm after the clearing, for its roots were not deep enough to hold it steady. But a tree that has been exposed to the tearing and pull of the wind from its early days has had to send down roots deep enough and strong enough to hold it.

So it is with us. We may be sheltered from the difficulties and hardness of life, surrounded by the comfort and security of friends and family. Like the trees in the clump, we have not had to send our roots deep. Like the fool who says, "there is no God," we laugh and go on our way. We ignore spiritual responsibilities and the need for deep water. And then comes catastrophe: the loss of those we hold dear, the failure of sup-posed "security." Without roots we are blown over in the storm.

The storms of life, like the storms of nature, come unex-pectedly and without warning. We are prepared for them in the many small crises and concerns of our daily life, and if we take care in these little times of stress to turn to God, acknowl-edging our dependence on him and seeking his help, we are in effect taking a firmer hold in him. We are being "rooted." And when the big storms come, the hurricanes, he will not let us go.

In the land of the living we ought to have a root. Let our root be there. That root is out of sight; its fruits may be seen, the root cannot be seen. Our root is our charity; our fruits are our works. It is needful that thy works proceed from charity; then is thy root in the land of the living.

St Augustine of Hippo

What a world! If a man wants a life of sensual excess he can have that tonight, with all the wild thrill and mad sense of liberation that he seeks. He can seize his passionate desire at once, and pay for it, it may be, long afterward. But a man who wants a Christian character that, like a well-rooted tree, holds its own against the storms of life and in the autumn bears fruit for his generation's help, cannot get that at once; he must pay for it first, and then get it.

Harry Emerson Fosdick

O God, who knowest us to be set in the midst of so many and great dangers, that by reason of the frailty of our nature we cannot always stand upright: Grant to us such strength and protection, as may support us in all dangers, and carry us through all temptations; through Jesus Christ our Lord. Amen.

Collect for the Fourth Sunday after the Epiphany,
Book of Common Prayer

The Green Leaf

Faced with a building lot stripped bare of native foliage and newly laid with sod grass, the average homeowner quickly learns the art of transplanting. Whether he goes to a nearby patch of woods or the local nursery, the rules are much the same: as little damage to the roots as possible, severe pruning, and lots of water.

The severe pruning, which amounts to as much as a third of the leafy area, is to compensate for root damage in the move. There is a fine relationship between roots and foliage. They grow together and support each other. They are interdependent. For while the roots supply water and minerals from the earth, the leaves in their turn supply the roots with vital elements from the air and sun. No green plant can grow without light.

Jesus said: "I am the Light of the World" (John 8:12). Without him we cannot hope to mature, to grow, to stay green and fresh.

If you take a plant out of the light, cover it up, and keep it from the sun, you will find that within a day or two it has turned yellow or white, and that soon after it dies. We have a wading pool in the garden for our children. It has to be moved every day or so because of the grass, and even then the damage is hardly believable. We left it once for three or four days and had to reseed the whole area.

And we are no different from the grass! If we turn from the Light to the works of darkness, we will die and our roots with us, as surely as the grass died under the wading pool.

Maintaining the relationship between roots and foliage is something that the plant does naturally. If a branch is knocked off a tree, it will respond with a vigorous outshoot of new growth. But if caterpillars attack it, eating the foliage that already exists and new buds as well, a corresponding amount of roots will eventually die, partly because of the lack of nutrients provided by the leaves and partly because there is no need for them to exist without the leaves.

In a sense, our good works correspond to the foliage of a tree. As a root set in the earth sends up shoots at the first opportunity, so our root in God (acknowledged or not) sends up shoots of goodness. All goodness comes from God. No man is good, but God alone is good.

And as the root set in the ground produces shoots and foliage, and the foliage in turn feeds the roots and stimulates new growth in them in a continuous cycle of growth, so our life in God, our root in him, produces good works and these in turn deepen our relationship with him. It is a cycle of growth: love of God first, and then love of our neighbour.

It is possible for a tree or bush to have too much foliage, or at least to have it in the wrong places. In the beginning it doesn't much matter that the leaves and branches should be close to the ground, for the tree is young and still small. But the branch of a tree does not become higher as a tree grows taller. It always remains in the same place. Consequently, the gardener who wishes a tall and stately tree in front of the house, instead of a squat and bushy one, will have to exercise a little care in pruning. Lower branches must be cut off regularly if a tree is to grow to its full height with the high spreading branches of maturity. And the suckers that frequently appear at the base of a tree have to be rooted out diligently.

In the same way, it is possible for us to have too many good works, and to have them in the wrong places. In the beginning of our Christian life, they may be appropriate and helpful. But as we grow and mature, it may be necessary to exercise the pruning shears on some of our activity. Certainly if God does this for us and we find that some field of useful activity is suddenly and inexplicably closed to us, we should not complain but, like the tree, attempt to grow a little taller.

I suppose the classic example of too much foliage in the wrong place is found in the story of Mary and Martha. And Martha's modern counterpart is the woman who gets so busy working on fund raising or other good causes that she's even too tired to go to church. It does happen. A wise woman once told me: "If you're too busy to pray, the good Lord never meant you to be that busy."

Even for those who never miss church on Sunday and who have a daily quiet time with God, it's a good thing to make an occasional but thoughtful assessment of one's use of time and ability. And if illness or family responsibilities shut us off from a useful activity, we do well to accept it as the pruning of God in our life. Taken thus, without resentment, it will help us to grow taller. We cannot help but grow. And we can be equally sure that some challenging and rewarding sphere of usefulness will be opened up to us as a result of this acceptance. Very often such new works are composed of activities that we had never before thought of undertaking. Perhaps we had never felt capable of doing them, and perhaps we had never thought of them as useful.

Whatever our condition in life, good works will be provided for us to do. "He has created us for a life of good works, which he has already prepared for us to do" (Eph 2:10). As the landscape gardener anticipates the mature (if future) size of a plant, before he even digs the hole to put it in, and carefully considers where he wants his shade to fall in twenty years' time, so God knows where he has put us and for what reason. We may have no more knowledge of his design, or our future growth, than the sapling has of its yet unbudded branches and the restful shade it is expected to provide in the years to come.

In the meantime, it is probably a good thing to note that the leaf at the top of the tree does not differ at all from those produced at the bottom. They are just the same in shape and color, and are indistinguishable as "upper" and "lower" leaves. I think that our good works have this same quality. The important thing about whatever we are doing is not what we do, but that God wants us to do it. The good works that come to hand as we mature in faith are not necessarily more spiritual or virtuous or admirable in themselves. They may in fact be much more menial or thankless tasks than we would willingly have undertaken in our earlier years. But, like Brother Lawrence, we may even scrub floors to the glory of God, and if that is what he wants us to do, then it is the only work from which we shall receive any true satisfaction at all.

> *Blessed is the man*
> *who walks not in the counsel of the wicked,*
> *nor stands in the way of sinners,*
>   *nor sits in the seat of scoffers;*
> *but his delight is in the law of the Lord,*
>   *and on his law he meditates day and night.*
> *He is like a tree*
>   *planted by streams of water,*
> *that yields its fruit in its season,*
>   *and its leaf does not wither.*

Psalm 1:1–3

You yourselves used to be in the darkness, but since you have become the Lord's people you are in the light. So you must live like people who belong to the light. For it is the light that brings a rich harvest of every kind of goodness, righteousness, and truth.

Ephesians 5:8,9

Without grace, I am nothing but a dry tree, a barren stock fit only for destruction. Therefore, O Lord, let your grace always lead and follow me, and keep me ever intent on good works, through your Son Jesus Christ. Amen.

Thomas à Kempis

Flower and Fruit

The green plants that grow on the earth are appreciated and cultivated by mankind for many different reasons — shade, beauty, food, and at the very basic level, soil conservation. Necessities need to come first, but when these have been seen to, man has always had an eye for beauty. For most plants, the flower is the chief expression of the glory of God's creation. When the woods are blooming with delicate white trilliums and wood violets, and the air is filled with the fragrance of the wild hawthorn bloom, who can refuse to rejoice? The most stubborn heart is lifted up in the springtime chorus.

We often talk about people "blossoming" when some new or unexpected talent appears, or even if they should become more open and loving in their day-to-day relationships. The implication is the same in every case — something has changed the picture. The person involved is still the same person but with something added, some new dimension.

When we "blossom" in this way we give glory to God just as the flowers do because we become more truly what we are supposed to be, we come closer to our true potential. If God has given us a talent for music or mathematics, we do him dishonour when we do not bring this gift to its full flowering.

Not everyone has the more spectacular gifts of intellect or athletic prowess, but everyone can have the gift of love. Of all the spiritual gifts, it is the most important. Love that flowers between a man and a woman, or between a parent and child, is a wonderful thing to see. But it is second to the love that can exist between God and his creatures.

A man who has learned to love God must be constantly telling or showing it in a hundred ways — and these, if you like, are "flowers." They express God's goodness to us, and they show forth his glory. One of the most appropriately named books in Christian literature is the first biography of St Francis of Assisi. *The Little Flowers of St Francis* really has nothing at all to do with flowers. It is simply a collection of the loving words and deeds of the saint — the taming of the wolf of Gubbio, the cleansing of a leper, the conversion of some lawless robbers. And what glory it gives to God in all this!

Flowers will be blooming for most of the summer in our gardens, but spring has a special place in nature because so many things come to life at once. After the cold dead winter we seem to need the extra wallop of scent and color.

We have our spiritual springtime too. Some people call it a conversion. It's the time when we first become truly aware of the love of God in our own lives. We respond to this with a warm uprush of emotion. We're thawed out, the sap is running, and like the buds on the trees we're bursting with joy. Everyone must be told about it; nothing is too hard for us to do.

Springtime does not last beyond its appointed time in nature, and it does not last spiritually either. It's a growing time, a wonderful time, but then like the plants we have to settle our roots and take things a little more easily. It's a help to understand what is happening.

The blossom precedes the fruit on all flowering plants and trees, and from the heart of the blossom comes the fruit. Blossomtime is a joy in itself. Who, having walked through an orchard in the spring, can forget the soft blush of pink and white petals or the fragrant air? Why do so many tourists flock to Washington at Easter to see the cherry blossoms?

Just so is the neophyte Christian, the new-born child of God. His radiance, joy, and faith hardly bear description. He walks in Beauty and can imagine nothing else. And yet, like the blossom, this fades. As the petal curls and drops, so the radiance fades and the joy dims, and even faith takes flight. But the fruit is growing.

The fruit of the spirit is love, joy, peace, patience, kindness, goodness, faithfulness, gentleness, and self-control (Gal 5:22). Like the fruit of nature, it does not appear at once when the blossom leaves, nor all at the same time. In fact, when the first radiance goes we are hardly aware that anything is left. But as time goes on, the first green fruits become visible. It is not yet time for harvest, but at least we know that they are growing. The important thing is for us to refuse to be discouraged by what looks like a setback. We too must persist until we bear fruit (Luke 8:15).

One of the interesting things about blossoms and fruit is that trees in bloom need to be pollinated. If an apple tree in bloom has no contact with other apple trees in bloom, there will be no apples. Christians cannot exist is isolation either. They need the fellowship of other Christians in order to produce this harvest of goodness. Of course, it is not necessary to have either an orchard in the one case or a large congregation in the other, but at least two or three gathered together (Matt 18:20).

It often happens, Philothea, that, in the fair spring-time of spiritual consolations, we become so absorbed in their abundant delights that we perform fewer good works; on the contrary, in the midst of spiritual dryness and desolation, finding ourselves deprived of pleasure in devotion, we perform more good works and produce more abundant fruit through the interior practice of penance, humility, self-contempt, resignation, and renunciation of self-love.

St Francis de Sales

For everything there is a season, and a time for every matter under heaven:
a time to be born, and a time to die;
a time to plant, and a time to pluck up what is planted.

Ecclesiastes 3:1, 2

Almighty God, who hast given us grace at this time with one accord to make our common supplications unto thee; and dost promise that when two or three are gathered together in thy name thou wilt grant their requests: Fulfil now, O Lord, the desires and petitions of thy servants, as may be most expedient for them; granting us in this world knowledge of thy truth, and in the world to come life everlasting. Amen.

Prayer of St Chrysostom

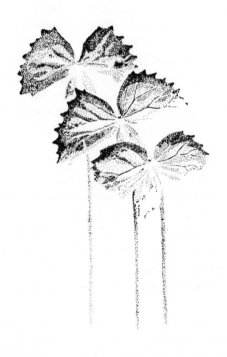

The Garden

When the three women went to the tomb on that first Easter morning, Mary saw Jesus but mistook him for the gardener. In the dimness of the early morning, it was a natural mistake.

But stop and think for a moment of what it means for the Lord to be the gardener in our lives. Up to now we have been thinking of plants and the way they grow. The sun shines and the rain falls on the just and the unjust alike (Matt 5:45). The principles of nourishment and growth are, in varying degrees, the same for all.

But there is a difference between a garden and the open fields and woods. There is a difference between the cultivated and the wild. Both have their own special beauty, but the wild-flower blooms and fades in a short time while the cultivated flower of the garden blooms more abundantly and bears more seed.

Garden flowers pay a price for their beauty. I pinch my seedlings off at the top in the spring to force a greater growth at the base, and consequently a greater bloom. The perennials are pruned regularly; some like the hydrangeas are cut right back to the ground every fall. They are not allowed the friendly company of weeds, and their roots must go deep because the surface is so frequently disturbed by the cultivator. The trees have their lower branches cut off every year to force them higher. And as for the roses! The care those ever-blooming beauties need is dreadful — a constant dusting, picking, and pruning.

And which of us is willing to go through that kind of treatment? Wouldn't we rather be wildflowers, left to our own devices to grow in the fields and woods?

The Old Testament prophets often spoke of Israel as the Lord's vineyard (Isa 5:1–7). In the same way today, we might think of the church as God's garden. A big garden, mind you, on a big estate with room for formal plantings and nooks of natural greenery. Those very formal gardens with fountains and planted designs and close-clipped hedges remind me of stately old churches and monasteries, with their beautiful music and carefully conducted worship. And then there is the "natural" approach to gardening, which takes advantage of already existing boulders and streams (or else imports them!) and lets all grow in a disorganized kind of profusion. And this in a sense is like the groups of Christians who insist on free prayer in their worship and enthusiastic singing. In either case, God is praised and glorified.

A garden, whether formal or natural, must be cared for, and even those natural plantings are not so easy to maintain as they look. The weeds that Jesus spoke about, the weeds of worldly desires and cares and frustrations, must all be pulled out. Of course, no gardener would expect his flower beds to weed themselves, but God does expect it of us because we have both hearts and minds. When occasionally he does a bit of weeding for us, we complain about falling on hard times and tend to take him to task for it. So he usually leaves it up to us to get rid of bad habits and bad companions.

The soil of a garden, the drainage, light, and shade are not usually the same wherever you go in it. The wise gardener takes all this into account before he plants. The rich soil, which is so good and necessary for many plants, leaves others with nothing but foliage. Nasturtiums, with their gorgeous orange and golden flowers, like a sandy soil and will not bloom in good black earth. Some plants tolerate shade well, while others can stand strong sun all day.

And as there are many different types of flowers, so there are many different types of Christians. What a dull garden it would be with nothing but marigolds!

Just occasionally, however, a gardener will put a sun-loving flower in a shady spot in the hope of brightening up a dark corner. Fortunately plants do their best and don't complain. A flower planted in such an uncongenial location will never win any prizes at the horticultural show, but if it produces any bloom at all, it is doing the job the gardener wanted it to do. He couldn't ask any more.

God treats us like that too. But we are not so patient under his hand as the flower. "If only I had his opportunity, or her freedom, or that job. . . ." Yes, given this or that or the other thing we might have produced beautiful blooms and been accounted a saint too. But this is not the way it works. We have to work out our salvation in the place where we are set and in the job which lies at hand. This is what the saints did; this is what made them saints. Joan of Arc could never have saved France if she had simply complained about not being a military man. After all, a shepherd girl is not in quite the same league, is she?

There are many saints who live and die unnoticed, as the flower in the dark spot is seldom noticed. But it is the gardener who must be pleased and no one else. God knows what darkness and drought each soul must endure, and it is he alone who will judge. As with the flower, so with us. Jesus taught that much would be expected from those who had been given much (Luke 12:48).

It takes all sorts to make a world; or a church. This may be even truer of a church. If grace perfects nature, it must expand all our natures into the full richness of the diversity which God intended when he made them, and heaven will display far more variety than hell. "One fold" doesn't mean "one pool." Cultivated roses and daffodils are no more alike than wild roses and daffodils.

C.S. Lewis

I realized, then, that all the flowers he has made are beautiful; the rose in its glory, the lily in its whiteness, don't rob the tiny violet of its sweet smell, or the daisy of its charming simplicity. I saw that if all these lesser blooms wanted to be roses instead, nature would lose the gaiety of her spring-tide dress — there would be no little flowers to make a pattern over the countryside. And so it is with the world of souls, which is his garden. He wanted to have great saints to be his lilies and roses, but he has made lesser saints as well; and these lesser ones must be content to rank as daisies and violets, lying at his feet and giving pleasure like that. Perfection consists simply in doing his will, and being just what he wants us to be.

St Therese of Lisieux

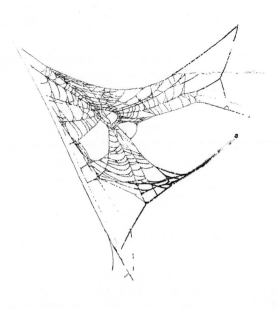

Fences

If we think of the church as God's garden, it might also be useful to consider that most gardens have some kind of fence around them. The church has a "fence" too — a fence made up of creeds and dogmas, articles of belief, statements of faith, and when you come right down to it, rules and regulations.

Probably nothing is in greater danger of being scrapped these days than these very formulas that make up the "fence" around the church. Nobody wants creeds; nobody wants rules. The general trend of the modern church is to be perfectly "open" to the world around it, without any definitive barriers of belief or practice.

But before we tear down the old fence and send it off to the junk yard, it might be worthwhile to consider why we have fences in the first place. If you have a garden, why do you fence it?

One of the interesting features of a brand-new suburban development is that there are no fences. The builders move in, clear the land if there are trees, stake out the lots and erect houses. When you move in, if you are lucky, there will be new-sodded grass but that will be it. There is only so much that one homeowner can do in one summer, so it may take a year or two before changes really become noticeable. People put in trees, shrubs, and do foundation planting around the house. Fences are more expensive to put up, and since they don't need time to grow, most people will leave them till the third or fourth summer, when suddenly they begin to multiply around the neighbourhood.

Fences are put up for protection and privacy, and in the case of large properties, as a boundary marker. People in the suburbs don't usually need the boundary marked by a fence because lines are straight and the distance is short, but if the owner of a large estate or a farmer had to have his property surveyed every time one of the neighbours decided to sell a piece of land, it could be a real headache as well as a major expense. Once the property has been surveyed, it ought to be marked out by a fence of some sort so that the same work won't have to be done over and over again.

Most of the surveyor's work, the setting of the boundaries of Christian faith and practice, was accomplished in the church in its very early years, and the foundation of the fence was put in by the early church councils as they worked over different lines of Christian thought, accepting some as doctrine and condemning others as heresy.

The farmers who first settled the part of the country where I live cleared fields that were overgrown with young trees or littered with glacier-strewn boulders. This had to be done before they could plough or plant. The trees and rocks that they cleared became the fences and boundary markers of their fields. Split-rail fences still zig-zag across the farmland, and rock walls separate one field from another.

This is how the church erected "fences" at the beginning. The difficulties and doubts, the rocks on the surface and later those that turned up in the ploughing, were sorted out and carefully heaped on the edge of the field. And through this sorting-out process, not only were the boundaries firmly established but the sometime hazards of the faith became in themselves a barricade and a defense against the non-Christian world.

This idea of a barricade and a defense is precisely what modern churchmen object to. They maintain that by erecting these barriers, the church keeps non-Christians on the outside, and equally prevents Christians within the church from becoming actively involved in the major social and political issues of our day.

One of my neighbours had a thing about fences, garden fences. There was nothing that she objected to more than a fence. She loved the early days in our neighbourhood when nobody at all had a fence and there was just one big field of uninterrupted grass, with a few boundary stakes stuck in here and there. Gradually the flower beds were put in, and not long after that the fences began going up. The reason was clear enough. Without some kind of fence, stray dogs would wander in and water the evergreens, and the neighbourhood children would trample down the peony sprouts in a far-ranging game of tag, and the rabbits from the nearby woods would come and eat all the lettuce heads in a single night. If you're going to have a real garden, you've got to have a fence! As for my neighbour who didn't like fences, let it be noted that she had no garden. She didn't want a fence because she had nothing to protect. The dogs ran as freely in her yard as they did in the abandoned fields nearby. There were no flowers, no shrubs, and even the grass was thin and dreary.

It is not surprising that the same people who complain about the sterility of contemporary faith are also the ones who have been tearing down the fences. You cannot keep a garden if you freely admit to it all the stray dogs and careless children of the neighbourhood. Jesus told us not to cast pearls before swine. I assume that he was talking about essentially the same matter. If you place something of value into the hands of those who have no concept of its value, then you might as well throw it away.

Fences are also put up for privacy. If you are going to have breakfast out in the garden, you don't really want the whole world watching you. If you plan to spend a hot afternoon sitting in the shade of your favourite tree with a glass in one hand and a book in the other, you don't really want to be dragged into the daily neighbourhood cocktail and gossip session. Small though the barrier may be, nevertheless it affords some protection for your private life.

The question, of course, is whether Christians in general, and the church in particular, have this right to privacy from the demands of a hurting world. Does not the church have a responsibility to share what it has with those in need?

When a gardener decides to put up a fence, he has a choice of two basic types — a wire or chain-link fence, supported on metal posts, or a so-called privacy fence, usually made of wood panels, which can be as high as eight feet. The first gives protection from the stray dogs and so on; the second gives the same protection, and also privacy from the outside world, but it does have a drawback. A wall, whether it is of wood or stone, which sticks eight feet up in the air is a barrier not only to curious eyes but also to the sun, and it will cast a long shadow. It seems that you cannot have your privacy and the full value of the sun.

The same distinction is, I think, true of the church. As Christians, we need the protection that a "fence" affords, but if we try to use these rules and regulations, these articles of belief, to separate and hide ourselves from those outside, then we will lose some of the sunshine of God's grace.

The beautiful garden is an inviting garden. Passers-by, who stop to admire the bloom on the roses or the lush display of dahlias, may wish for an invitation to come into the garden so that they can see it a little more closely. If they can see from outside that it is a place of beauty, they will long to go into it. Some may enter the high-walled garden, the garden with the "privacy" fence, through curiosity, but fear of the unknown will keep many more outside.

And so it is with the church. "Christianity is caught, not taught." It is chiefly through exposure to other Christians, and not by hints about the mysteries, that conversions take place. Christians cannot afford the luxury of privacy in their faith. If we believe in God, we must say so, and every action must show it.

The garden of the church is not an exclusive garden. Anyone is welcome to enter; anyone is welcome to stay. But there is only one way to enter — by the gate; and there is only one way to stay — by being planted. Jesus said that he was the gate. We must come by him; we must accept him as the Lord of our lives. And Jesus said that the Father would have to plant us, for "every plant which my Father in heaven did not plant will be pulled up" (Matt 15:13). We cannot blow in over the fence like a seed on the wind; we cannot drift in "by accident." We must come by the gate and be planted.

God cultivateth thee, that thou mayest be fruitful; and thou worshippest God, that thou mayest be fruitful. It is good for thee that God cultivateth thee; it is good for thee that thou worshippest God. If God the cultivator depart from man, man is abandoned; if man the worshipper depart from God, it is the man himself who is abandoned. God neither increaseth by thy approach to him, nor decreaseth by thy withdrawal. He then will be our possession, that he may find us; we shall be his possession, that he may rule us.

St Augustine of Hippo

Cheap grace is the preaching of forgiveness without requiring repentance, baptism without church discipline, communion without confession, absolution without contrition. . . . Costly grace is the gospel which must be sought again and again, the gift which must be asked for, the door at which a man must knock. . . . Costly grace is the sanctuary of God; it has to be protected from the world, and not thrown to the dogs.

Dietrich Bonhoeffer

Seedtime and Harvest

The normal and instinctive goal of every plant is to produce seed, and as far as the plant is concerned, flowers and fruit are only a by-product of this goal. But the gardener does not give up his precious flower beds to a plant that has nothing more than this to commend it. Reproducing itself by growing seed is not enough!

The distinction between weeds and other garden plants is completely arbitrary. If a plant produces flowers that are pleasant to see, or if some part of it is good to eat, or if it grows tall to provide shelter and shade, then it is worth keeping and cultivating. Otherwise, it will generally be known as a weed, useless and good-for-nothing.

This instinct of the plants to produce seed is at least roughly equivalent to the basic and God-given instincts of mankind, which are directed toward self-preservation and preservation of the species. And just as a plant that fulfilled *only* its instinct to produce seed would be simply a weed, so a man who follows his instincts, with no other grace to commend him, is little better than an animal. At the grassroots level, the man who has the opportunity and ability to help his neighbour, but insists on following his instinctive drive for success, is on a plane with a fast-bolting lettuce. To say that someone has "gone to seed" is a derogatory term simply because so many good plants have been lost to the harvest when this happens.

Just as there are some people who claim that all instincts are right and proper and must be fulfilled, so there are some people who claim the opposite and say that no instincts are right and proper. Yet neither group has grasped the truth, for it is a strange fact that we never talk about peas and corn and cucumbers "going to seed." Instead we say that they have been fruitful. It all depends on what kind of plant we are talking about.

All plants have the same necessary parts: roots, stem, leaves, flowers, fruit, and seed. But it is generally true that *one* of these will become the outstanding feature of the plant, the reason for which it is grown and cultivated. No one in his right mind would grow potatoes for their leaves, or tomatoes for their roots! This does not excuse the potato from having leaves, nor the tomato from having roots. On the contrary, they are a necessary part of the plant in order for it to fulfill its purpose, although potato leaves and tomato roots are not in themselves a very good reason for the plants' existence.

People are like this too. St Paul wrote to the Corinthians that God gives each man a different gift as he wishes. It may be a gift of wisdom or teaching or faith or power to heal. It may be something else. But it is a gift that God gives in accordance with his will for each one of us. The possessor of such a gift does himself and the Giver a disservice when he thinks the gift is all-important. It must inevitably become the expression of his personality, as the long full root is the expression of a carrot, but it cannot be his total function.

The essential relationship for every plant lies in the interaction of root and leaves. For people it lies in the interaction of love for God and love for our neighbour. One love should feed the other, as roots feed leaves and leaves nourish roots. One cannot be neglected without the other suffering.

The only real heresies in Christianity come from a lack of love. The church has suffered many pseudo-saints who have possessed an overpowering "love" for God but who were uncommonly cantankerous when it came to dealing with ordinary mortals. St John asked how a man could love God, whom he had not seen, when he did not love his brother whom he had seen (1 John 4:20). Such a man would be like a root vegetable that decided it would put all its energy into being a root! Could anything be more ridiculous?

At the other extreme is the Christian who expresses all of his love to God through loving his neighbour. He has no time for worship or prayer, but goes about doing good in a ceaseless round of activity. And he is like any leafy plant that decides to do without its root! The strange thing is that people like this can keep going for such a long time before it begins to show. They are rather like carrots and beets pulled fresh out of the garden. The tops will continue to drain stored moisture and nourishment from the root, and they may stay green for several days even though they are no longer planted firmly in the ground.

Within this framework of love, there is always a remarkable variety of expression, just as there is a variety of vegetables and fruit and flowers in any well-ordered garden. And God arranges for certain gifts to flower and find expression in certain times and places, just as the gardener arranges for his floral displays and the farmer plans for harvest.

It would be nice to think that we could cooperate with God to produce beauty and goodness in the world just as the plants cooperate with the gardener. Willful and self-centered creatures that we are, we seem to be able to do this only by grace and not by nature. It may not be particularly comforting but it should be helpful to consider that the plants do in fact normally present exactly the same problem to the gardener. The vegetable is, I think, a perfect small example of this.

Annual plants like vegetables usually have only one end in view — to produce seed. From the gardener's point of view, this may be of interest and it may not. It depends on why he is growing the vegetable in question. Although the production of seed is the instinctive goal of the plant, it may not be its proper end. The proper end of lettuce, for instance, is in a salad. If it is allowed to "bolt," to produce seed, it will be ruined for its true function in life. The same is true of beets and carrots and spinach and cabbage. The gardener sees to his harvest and allows these vegetables to produce only as much seed as he needs for next year's garden.

This is not to say that producing seed is wrong. Some plants only find their true function in life as they follow this same instinct to produce seed. Most fruit — tomatoes, oranges, apples, and so on — is only a container for the plant's seed, but without the seed, the plant would not have produced the fruit. And then again, in some plants like peas and corn, it is the seed itself that is valuable.

The real problem is that what is true for one man is not necessarily true for another. Except for the call to love God and our neighbour, there is no universal vocation, and unlike the plants in the vegetable garden, we are not all neatly lined up in a row with a paper at the end to say what we are.

There are those who, like the beets and carrots, have the best part of their lives hidden in the "ground," that is, in the love of God. The full value of their life will not be known until the final harvest, and in the meantime, those who do not recognize the leafy form of beets and carrots are rather inclined to dismiss them as useless additions to the vegetable patch.

Others may be called more obviously to a sacrificial life of good works, which again does not allow for any more fulfillment of instinct than is given a lettuce or cabbage. No matter — for what distinguishes mankind from the animals is not instinct but purpose of life.

There are more plants in the garden than root and leafy vegetables, and most of them are allowed to produce seed, even though it may still be incidental to the gardener's purpose. Melons, cucumbers, tomatoes, apples, and almost every kind of fruit carry their seeds within them, and these may be eaten or discarded according to their size or flavour. A necessary evil, one might be inclined to feel, and yet it does seem that whenever seedless varieties of any fruit are developed, they never have quite the same richness of flavour as their seed-bearing cousins.

For the flower and fruit alike, for the artist and the plumber, the true course of living will most often run in the normal paths of work and friends and family. And these in their turn will add taste and flavour to the fruit. How else can we learn patience without being kept waiting? Or receive peace without turmoil? Or joy without sorrow? How can we develop self-control unless we are tested?

Lastly, there are plants that are grown for their seed — peas, corn, beans, wheat. It is the seed that is important. By a special gift, the instinct of the plant to produce seed is turned into a positive good over and above mere reproduction. There are people like this too — doctors, teachers, farmers, mothers, and so on — whose work may be motivated by the need to earn a living and raise a family, but who bring to it a quality of love and joy and concern that utterly transcends the grosser elements of greedy self.

Where do you and I fit into all this? Life is more complicated for us than for the plants. We do not come neatly labeled. We are not easily classified, and we may combine the characteristics of more than one type of life, but perhaps the comparison will help us to understand something of our necessarily different natures.

What all this says about us chiefly is that our instincts, though given us for a purpose, do not always need to be gratified in order for us to find fulfillment. Following our instincts may be right and proper, but it is not the place of our instinct to tell us so. This is the work of the Holy Spirit, and it is only when we lay our hearts and minds and wills open to his guidance that we are able to complete our true purpose in life, and in doing this to find fulfillment.

Personal Christianity is a profound relationship between the soul and God, and its innermost expression, as Jesus said, comes in solitude in a chamber with the door shut. If someone says that the inner relationship with the divine is the very root of all Christian experience, I agree. But that is just what it is — the root, the invisible, underground, vital root; but it is not the fruit; and any Christian that tries to be all root is just as much a failure as a tree would be that tried the same impossibility.

Harry Emerson Fosdick

A tree gives glory to God first of all by being a tree. For in being what God means it to be, it is imitating an idea which is in God and which is not distinct from the essence of God, and therefore a tree imitates God by being a tree. . . . Unlike the animals and the trees, it is not enough for us to be individual men. For us, holiness is more than humanity. If we are never anything but men, never anything but our natural selves, we will not be saints and we will not be able to offer to God the worship of our imitation, which is sanctity.

Thomas Merton

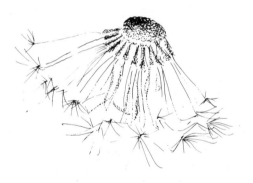

Stakes and Supports

In the normal course of nature's economy, plants that are meant to stand upright are provided with a strong stem, thick enough and hard enough to withstand the force of the wind and the rain. The observable rule is that the taller bushy plants have dry and woody stems, while the juicy easily snapped stems belong to new growth and low-lying flowers.

But there are exceptions to every rule. Some plants need staking: tomatoes, beans, peas. They grow upright at first, but later the weight of their fruit will pull them down if they have no support.

I set out a dozen tomato plants one summer but didn't get around to putting in the stakes the same day. Then with one small domestic crisis after another, I never did get around to it, and we managed to go off on our summer holidays without a backward glance at the tomato patch. We were away for a month, and when we came back the plants were a mess! They had continued to grow, but vinelike across the ground, all tangled into each other with lots of leaves and very little fruit. What fruit there was lay on the ground exposed to the damp and every bug that walked past. Fruit was rotting that had not even ripened, and although I was able to salvage parts of the crop, there wasn't one whole tomato in the bunch.

Now from nature's point of view, this was okay. Fruit is meant to produce seed for reproduction, and rotting tomatoes help to spread out the seed. But from the gardener's point of view, it's a disaster. After all, he wants to eat the fruit.

Staking tomatoes and similar plants helps them produce a good crop, and I think many of us need a similar support in our spiritual lives if we are going to bear any worthwhile fruit. We all need to undertake some form of self-discipline, some external rules, which will help us to live, not just according to the way we feel, but according to the way we know we ought to live.

The old spiritual writers used to talk about a *rule of life*, which was simply an individual's promise to God that he would try to do on a regular basis certain things that he knew he ought to do. This may involve a daily Bible reading and prayer time, as well as weekly attendance at church. It may be hard or easy, depending on the ability and desire of the person adopting the rule. The point to keep in mind, however, is that a rule is not something to aim at, but something to do. It is important to be realistic about one's abilities to carry out such a program.

We all have experiences with broken New Year's resolutions, and probably the biggest reason for the high breakage rate is the universal attempt to take on more than we can handle. You cannot tie up all of the tomato plant to its stake at one time — you can only tie it as it grows! We are just the same. As we develop spiritually, we are able to take on a bit more and a bit more, but only as we grow.

Many people think such a rule of life is a piece of old-fashioned nonsense, not unlike the Victorian backboard. They argue that it detracts from the ease that we ought normally to have in our religious practices, and that it will make us stiff and unnatural. And they have a point — there are some people who get so wrapped up in their "rule" that it becomes all-important and they forget why they have a rule in the first place. Jesus talked about people like this in the story of the good Samaritan: the priest and the Levite were engrossed with their personal "rule" (not to defile themselves with blood before going to the temple), and so they missed out on what was more important.

But if a rule is taken as a support and not as an end in itself, it will help us grow into the kind of people we really want to be. We will be no more unnatural or stiff about it than the tomato plant tied to its stake. Whether a tomato plant is bound to the stake with ties or bound to the ground with its weight, it is bound. And the healthier-looking plant is the one that has been trained to grow on the stake.

The idea of training is not a very comfortable thought, nor is it very comfortable in actual practice until the training has so done its work that we cannot be comfortable in any other way. The man who has had a morning quiet time every day for twenty years will be less likely to miss it than the man who has only been at it for three months, not because he finds it more enjoyable but simply because this has become part of the pattern of his life.

Apart from the soft-stemmed plants, there are others that need support too. Young saplings need a stake when they are first planted to keep them standing straight in the wind. Later their stems will harden and they will be able to take the full force of the gale without any support, but in the beginning they too need training.

One of the more unusual ways of staking and training trees is called *espaliering*. In this case the young tree will be planted right up against a wall or a frame support, and it will then be trained to grow quite flat. The branches are securely fastened to the support, and new growth is either fastened in similar fashion or mercilessly pruned. The training normally gives the tree a completely symmetrical form, and although it may be highly unnatural, it is also extremely attractive in an ornamental garden.

In a similar vein, I think many Christians have been called at different times to particularly difficult vocations. There is nothing "natural" about this. The paths they followed were in response to an individual call from God, and the saints who answered were the first to say that the call was not for everyone. Their training lay as much in the hands of God as the apple tree set out for espaliering lies in the hands of the gardener. Being human, we tend to wonder about this and perhaps to criticize, just as the apple tree in an orchard might wonder about the "special" tree being grown in the garden.

The espaliered apple tree may not bear any better than the trees in the orchard, but its fruit will have one distinct quality. Because each branch stands out on its own, with no other branches to shade it from the sun, all of the fruit will have the benefits of the sun's ripening rays. There will be no little green apples tucked away under masses of foliage.

This mass exposure to the sun is in some ways incidental to the gardener's purpose in having an espaliered tree. Given the apple's upright stem, the same effect can be achieved by the simpler process of judicious pruning. In the case of tomatoes, however, exposure to the sun is one of the chief objectives of the staking.

In the same way, if we undertake a rule of life, it is because we want to grow in a certain way. As we turn our thoughts back again and again to God and force ourselves into loving and thankful habits of mind, we are training an upright stem. There will be days when the heat is fierce and we would love to sink into the coolness of the ground, but like the tomato we are held by the ties of our "rule," our agreement with God. So we go on, and as we persist, the fruit of our lives, the fruits of gentleness and patience and love, will grow and ripen and become very sweet.

I think everyone has to have some minimum rule of prayer, not too ambitious, rather below our powers, but something we will keep regularly and really seriously and will go on with through thick and thin. Adjust it if it does not clothe your spirit. Review your plan afresh. Having said this, I am sure that more people pray than think they do. Some people find that a rule positively acts as an inhibition to them. If they offer their rule to God as something kept not for our own sakes but as a garden enclosed, a trellis on which the

living thing grows, it is well. But do not despise the little lift-
ings up of the heart as you go about. . . . We need rule and
suppleness, discipline and freedom, structure, and living
shoots of growth.

Edward Keble Talbot

I bind unto myself to-day
The power of God to hold and lead,
His eye to watch, his might to stay,
His ear to hearken to my need.
The wisdom of my God to teach,
His hand to guide, his shield to ward;
The word of God to give me speech,
His heavenly host to be my guard.

Saint Patrick's Breastplate

The Compost Heap

One of the loveliest scents of autumn is the smell of burning leaves. It calls forth all kinds of nostalgia about the past summer, and other summers and other falls. Raking the leaves is no great joy in itself, but jumping into the huge pile was always fun, even though they scattered and had to be raked again for the final burning.

My children are missing this joy. No one in our neighbourhood burns leaves. We don't even rake leaves. We don't have any trees! We're trying to grow them, but it takes an awfully long time before a young tree has enough leaves to bother raking, and even longer before there's a big enough pile to bother burning.

Actually, good gardeners don't burn leaves anyway. They pile them into a compost heap. Fallen leaves are the gardener's gold, a rich source of organic nutrition returning to the soil. The rich topsoil we value is rich precisely because of the dead vegetation and dried leaves that have been absorbed into it. Observe a fallen leaf on the ground, how the green and yellow disappear to be replaced by dull black as damp and decay do their work, and you will see why black earth is black. Years of fallen leaves have been dissolved by time and worked by roots and worms into the one rich composition.

Our good works are a little like the leaves on a tree, and like the leaves on a tree, they do not last. One of the hardest lessons to learn in life is how to let go when you have finished a particular piece of work. The time has come for you to move to something else, and perhaps another is given the job of continuing what you had begun. Because he is a different person, the work will be changed in its character and scope. Only God is changeless. We change; what we do changes, and it changes even more if somebody else begins to do it.

There are two things that are particularly hard to take when this happens. The worst thing that can happen is to see one of our former projects so completely bungled by a successor that it fails altogether. This is awful, and there is hardly anybody who hasn't had the experience in one degree or another. It may only have been a particular kind of fund-raising event for the hospital that you ran very successfully the previous year. The new committee did everything wrong, and you would love to say so (although obviously you can't!). What they say is that the whole scheme is impracticable anyway, and that next year they're going to be a lot more realistic and try something simple.

It's bad enough learning to accept change when it comes in this nitty-gritty committee way, but it can be soul-destroying when it attacks something for which you really care. Take the case of a minister, social worker, teacher, or politician who has poured years of his life into a particular cause or reform, and then sees it wiped out the instant he moves or retires. It's not a case of beginning again; it's a matter of seeing what amounts to a life's work disappear before your eyes. And yet the disappearance is only apparent.

The leaves also seem to disappear. They are out of sight, and yet the good they do goes on working in a new way. We cannot judge by what we see. The work we do involves God and the people we deal with. We can struggle to build up organizations and structures and laws, but we do so only to reach another goal. We cannot expect these forms to last. What counts is the work we do today, and if we do it faithfully, God will see to it that this work goes on to provide a rich compost for future generations.

The second difficult thing that can happen to an old project is to have our successor turn it into a smashing success after we had left it in apparent failure. There are hundreds of stories like this — missionaries who struggled for many years without a single convert; political leaders who were put out of office because of their reforms, only to have them taken up by the opposition. The child in us cries out, "It isn't fair!" And it isn't fair. But who said life was fair? Life brings humbling and unexpected turns at each corner, and if we do not resist them in bitterness, they will bring us closer to God.

Here again we have to trust that the work we did before in honesty and godly service is being used by God now. Another may get the credit, but the glory belongs to God alone. Our leaves have fallen and been used to enrich the earth where our successor flourishes. We do not and cannot work alone; we live on the prayers and work of those who have gone before us.

At the Cape Cod National Seashore there are some interesting nature walks explaining the ecology of the peninsula. One of these leads down into a white cedar swamp. The cedar is extremely resistant to water rot, and so when a swampy stretch is able to support any trees at all, the white cedar is one of the first to grow there. Each year it sheds some of its foliage, and this settles on the swampland so that it gradually builds up and fills in. As the swamp becomes firmer, maple trees begin to grow and shed their heavy foliage at an even faster rate, until at last the swampland is no longer a swamp and other varieties of trees are able to move in. Eventually these faster growing trees take over the whole stretch of land, and the slow-growing cedars are cut out of the land that had been theirs.

The story is repeated in other places and other ways. In Florida the mangrove tree is known as the "land-builder" because, settling into a sandbank, its long roots trap the shifting sand beneath and its thick foliage falls from above to make a compost. When the land is finally firm, other trees will grow on what the mangrove built.

This happens to us. Someone else will build, knowingly or not, on the work we did. We are all dependent on each other. There is another side to the coin too. It may be that you are the one who comes in as a successful replacement. The temptation is to be proud of our success when this happens, and so we have to be strong to remember that what we apparently have done on our own may in fact be the result of years of prayer by someone quite unknown to us, or years of work by those who have gone on before us. We sometimes harvest what others have sown.

St Paul says what really matters is God. "Each one of us does the work the Lord gave him to do: I planted the seed, Apollos watered the plant, but it was God who made the plant grow. The one who plants and the one who waters really do not matter. It is God who matters, for he makes the plant grow" (1 Cor 3:5, 6).

Nature's compost is a little bit different from the pile in the garden. Unless you have so many leaves that you just don't know what to do with them, the compost pile also gets all the little bits of green stuff that would otherwise go into the garbage — wilted lettuce, leftover green beans, grass clippings, hedge trimmings, and so on. It's a real lesson in nature's economy to see how waste material can be transformed into something valuable. And compost is valuable. Dug into the flower beds as a soil conditioner or used as a mulch to keep down weeds, it also provides valuable nutrients for the plants it surrounds.

We don't like to think of our good works as "waste material," much less as "garbage." We are clothed and surrounded by them as a tree is clothed in its leaves. Yet just as the tree must lose its leaves and stand bare before the winter wind, so we also must face our Lord's coming without the covering of our good works. They were necessary to our growth, as the leaves were necessary to the tree, but in the last analysis they don't count.

What counts is our faith in God and our love for him. Our good works helped us to grow strong in this, just as the leaves did their part in helping the roots and the tree to grow stronger. But we have to remember that they don't count, for "a man is put right with God only through faith, and not by doing what the law commands" (Rom 3:28).

As a Jew, St Paul had everything going for him: the right external ceremonies had been performed at the right time, and inwardly, by his own reckoning, he was zealous and without fault. And yet he says he threw them all away in order to gain Christ. As a Christian, Paul gave himself completely to the work of an apostle, with all its hardship and suffering, acknowledging all along that these counted for nothing. He did not hang on to his "works" but let them fall from him, as the leaves fall from the tree. Who can tell how many plants have sprung up in the fertile compost that he and so many others have left?

We have all become like one who is unclean,
  and all our righteous deeds are like a polluted garment.
We all fade like a leaf,
  and our iniquities, like the wind, take us away.

Isaiah 64:6

I reckon everything as complete loss for the sake of what is so much more valuable, the knowledge of Christ Jesus my Lord. For his sake I have thrown everything away; I consider it all as mere garbage, so that I might gain Christ, and be completely united with him.

Philippians 3:8

O God, when our use of this world is over and we make room for others, may we not leave anything ravished by our greed or spoiled by our ignorance, but may we hand on our common heritage fairer and sweeter through our use of it. Amen.

Walter Rauschenbusch

Fertilizer

Apart from the actual planting and cultivation of flowers, the gardener has a number of other methods he employs to improve both the size and quality of his plants. The use of fertilizer is one of the most common gardening devices, even among relatively inexperienced gardeners.

But fertilizer can be dangerous. It must be given in the right amounts or the roots may be burned. It must be given in the right season or the plant may grow beyond its strength. A big plant can take more fertilizer than a small one. In fact, a big plant needs more fertilizer.

God gives us a kind of fertilizer, a help to stimulate growth. And like the plants, the bigger and stronger we grow, the more we have need of it. In a sense, it is like time spent in his presence or waiting upon him, or even a more direct calling upon his part. What would kill interest in one man, or perhaps scare him off, would hardly meet the need and desire of another.

Somehow in this modern world we have lost the whole concept and idea of silence. We long for peace and quiet, and we don't know what to do with it when we get it! Most businesses operate amid a jangle of telephones, typewriters, and taped stereo music, while housewives do their work listening to the radio hot-lines and TV soap operas.

Now it is quite possible to work in the middle of such a hubbub and to maintain a center of quiet within oneself. We do in some ways become conditioned to the noise. But it is not very easy. It is for this reason that monks and nuns have separated themselves from the "world" in the past and in the present too. They hope that by practicing an exterior silence they will find it easier to maintain inner silence before God and to build up a habit of quiet thought and recollection.

God is not rude. He does not interrupt us in our busy life, and if we prefer to be occupied with something or someone else, he leaves us to it. If we turn to him, he is always ready for us, but except under very extraordinary circumstances, he will not burst in upon our privacy.

When we realize this fact, it becomes imperative that we should deliberately set aside at least some regular time to be with him. For the majority of people, this time may be just that one hour a week on Sunday morning. For others, there may be also a regular time of prayer each day. But in all of this, we are rushed and hurried. The roast is shoved in the oven just before we leave for church; our morning quiet time is cut short by our oversleeping or a crying child. We are seldom really quiet.

A retreat or "quiet day" is probably the easiest way for the beginner to achieve some kind of silence. Having no one else to talk with, we are forced by circumstances to renew acquaintance with our first Friend, and all the addresses and reading are intended to direct our thoughts to him as well.

God gives us something in this silence, and it is a little like fertilizer for the plants. With the flowers and trees, a dose of fertilizer is not immediately obvious. It sinks into the ground and goes to work rather slowly on the roots. It may be several weeks before the first results are seen and months before the last effects are felt.

A good retreat, like any kind of good prayer, cannot be measured by immediate results. We may experience a sense of well-being and closeness to God, but we are seldom aware of what is *really* happening. What God does to and for us does not depend upon our understanding it or our realization of it, but upon our willingness for him to do it.

And like fertilizer, God's grace works in us, on the root. It may be weeks or months before the new growth is first obvious to ourselves and others in our conscious thoughts and actions.

To preserve the silence within — amid all the noise. To remain open and quiet, a moist humus in the fertile darkness where the rain falls and the grain ripens — no matter how many tramp across the parade-ground in whirling dust under an arid sky.

Dag Hammerskjöld

And when we turn to the inner circle of the spiritual masters — the men and women, not necessarily gifted or distinguished, to whom God was "a living, bright reality" which supernaturalized their everyday life and transmuted their homeliest actions into sublime worship — we find that their roots struck deep into the soil of spiritual silence.

E. Herman

Thus we see that silence, which is so important in our growth in newness of life, is no negative barren condition, but the intense activity of creative love, the breath of God at work in the garden of the soul.

Estelle C. Carver

The Gardener's Craft

There is another ancient technique that only the experienced gardener uses. It is called grafting. In this process the roots of one plant are joined to the woody stem of another stronger plant (usually of the same species) in order to produce a superior quality of bloom or fruit.

Apple trees are probably the best example of this. Brought into cultivation from wild trees thousands of years ago, apples are one of the oldest fruits known to man. It was traditionally an apple that Eve ate and gave to Adam! We know good apples by names like McIntosh, Baldwin, Delicious, Winesap, and so on. But all these different varieties are held constant in shape and taste and texture only through the process of grafting. Their goodness cannot be reproduced by seed. If you plant the seeds of your favorite apple, the fruit of the tree which grows will probably be small and sour.

We live in McIntosh country, and in the fall the roadside stands are heaped with bushel baskets of that round sweet fruit. The original McIntosh tree was discovered by an Ontario farmer (named McIntosh) over a century ago. It was just a wild tree in the field, but its fruit was good. Buds, or young shoots, were taken from it and grafted to the roots of seedling apple trees. And every McIntosh apple tree since has been created through that same process of grafting in order to keep the mysterious link, carried in the wood from that first McIntosh apple tree.

Now think what this means in terms of conversion. Jesus said that unless a man is born again, he cannot enter the kingdom of God (John 3:3). Isn't the wild apple tree born again when it receives the graft of good fruit-bearing wood? St Paul says much the same thing: "I have been crucified with Christ; it is no longer I who live but Christ who lives in me" (Gal 2:20).

We are called to be Christians — "little Christs" — just as the wild young apple tree is called by the farmer to become a McIntosh. And if we succeed in bearing good fruit, it is not our doing. We can take no credit. It is because Christ has been grafted in us as the wood of the good apple tree has been grafted in the wild.

And for all this we maintain our individuality. McIntosh trees are known by their fruit (as are we!), but otherwise they look like any other apple tree. Every tree in an orchard has a different shape and is dependent upon its own roots for nourishment. Some grow more quickly and strongly than others, and some produce more abundantly. In essence, a McIntosh tree has all the freedom it can have within the limits of "apple-treehood."

I've heard it said that God has no grandchildren. This again is like the apple tree. As the McIntosh cannot of its own seed produce good apple trees, so we cannot be sure that our children will grow up to love God. Christ must be grafted into the heart of each person, just as good apple wood must be grafted into each tree.

Probably the most graphic example of this grafting process is provided for us within the context of Holy Communion. We are invited to partake of the body and blood of our Lord in order that he may abide in us, and we in him. The apple tree can be grafted in one fell swoop. But we human beings are much more complicated creatures. Even a skin graft is a long and painful process, and how much more difficult and delicate must be the operation of the Holy Spirit on our inmost being.

Sometimes a graft doesn't take very well. We have two apple trees in the garden. One is doing well with good strong branches and lots of fruit. The other is having trouble with suckers.

I dig them out, but they sap the strength of the tree. If I were to let them grow, the graft would die completely and the new tree which grew from the suckers would not have the sweet fruit I want.

We are often like this too. We let the suckers of pride and self-will take over in our hearts. At the very least, they slow our growth, and if allowed to gain control, the graft is lost. Even the apple tree can reject a graft. How much more easily we can say no to God!

To have good fruit you must have a healthy tree; if you have a poor tree you will have bad fruit. For a tree is known by the kind of fruit it bears. You snakes — how can you say good things when you are evil? For the mouth speaks what the heart is full of. A good man brings good things out of his treasure of good things; a bad man brings bad things out of his treasure of bad things.

Matthew 12:33–35

There have been many whose lives have been full of thorns, but by believing on the Lord Jesus Christ they have become fruitful. I saw a tree on the mountain once, full of thorns. The man in charge said, "I can change this into a fruitful tree." How could it be done? A few years afterward I went to see it. The gardener had grafted it, and instead of the thorns there was excellent fruit. So the gracious Lord takes us in hand and makes us produce fruit. The Lord came for all, and he can turn sinners into saints, just as in the case of the tree I mentioned.

Sadhu Sundar Singh

Lord of all power and might, who art the author and giver of all good things: Graft in our hearts the love of thy Name, increase in us true religion, nourish us with all goodness, and of thy great mercy keep us in the same; through Jesus Christ our Lord. Amen.

Collect for the Seventh Sunday after Trinity,
Book of Common Prayer

Garden Pests

There is no garden that does not have its share of those little pests that chew on the stem and leaves of a plant, or lay their eggs in its fruit and destroy it. Garden bugs come in many shapes and forms, but they are almost universally the enemy of any well-kept garden.

The easiest way to get rid of them is to spray or dust the plants with a poisonous chemical, which will kill the insects and their eggs. Modern methods of insect control have made all the difference to the production of food in this hungry world. Crops that used to be vulnerable to the ravages of an insect invasion can now be protected by the use of appropriate pesticides.

For some years, gardeners have thought that was all there was to it. More recently, naturalists have been claiming and proving that, by the wholesale use of such chemicals as DDT, we have in effect been poisoning not only the insects but our whole environment. In the long run we poison ourselves.

Many naturalists, and even some gardeners, have gone so far as to suggest that we drop the use of pesticides entirely because in poisoning the insects we are also poisoning their natural enemies — the birds. If they go too, we will not be any better off in the end. No poison can reach all the insects, while birds can do a very effective job. Some baby birds will eat their own weight in food, mostly insects, every day. As they grow older, most of the smaller birds maintain an appetite that is proportionately three times larger than that of an adult working man's. A garden with a lot of birds can be kept relatively free of insects.

Beelzebub is an Old Testament name for the devil, and it means "Lord of the Flies." It is not hard to imagine all those vices and sins that trouble us as do flies or insects, creeping and crawling, hiding in the dark, chewing on root and stem, leaving behind a wake of destruction and rot. Lord of the flies, indeed. Lord of the borer and weevil and slug.

As in the garden, there are two possible approaches. There is poison, and there are birds.

To poison the bugs is to concentrate on eliminating them, which is surely a worthwhile objective. But eliminating sins is not much easier than eliminating insects. They have a way of coming back, of adapting themselves to the environment. We have rules laid down for us, or we lay them down for ourselves. "Thou shalt do no murder." "Thou shalt not steal." We accept these rules and add others. No smoking. No drinking. No lipstick. No movies. It's really quite simple. We poison those actions that lead us into sin by the simple act of setting them into terms of religious law. The well brought-up Puritan may be incapable of distinguishing the difference between lying and lipstick.

And like the DDT, these rules go on to poison our whole environment. Who can tell how much heartbreak was caused within the marriage vows by the poisonous attitude of the Puritan view of sex? Who knows how much hatred of Sunday was caused by that poisonous view of the restrictive Sabbath (no games, no laughing, no novels)?

None of this eliminates the problem. Like the insects, sin recurs again and again. It doesn't matter how hard the restrictions, or how vigorously we apply them. The effect of the law on sin is transitory, like the effect of poison on insects, and if we persist in trying to get rid of sin in this way, the poison will only sink deep and cause us trouble later on, like the DDT.

There have been times in our society when the Puritan ethic has taken over so completely as to shape the laws of the country.

There have been attempts at prohibition and censorship, yet in the end they failed. And the failure brought with it a licentiousness stronger than that which had been put down. Insects have been known to develop a resistance to certain poisons after awhile, and in the end they too are stronger than before.

The alternative to poison is birds. They are not so easy to handle as poison; they do not come at our beck and call. But once they are firmly established in a garden, they will stay unless something drives them away. There are ways of attracting birds — a bit of suet, trees that produce berries, a birdbath, and a few well-spaced birdhouses. When I was a child, we had no birds in our small yard until we set out to attract them in this way. The first summer we had plenty of visitors, and the next spring a pair of white-breasted swallows moved into our birdhouse. They came back every year after that, building nests and producing babies. There is no way of knowing how many insects they rid us of, but once the eggs were hatched the parents spent many anxious hours scurrying back and forth to the nest with grubs and flies for the hungry babies. We had a small vegetable garden, as well as flowers and fruit trees, but I never remember there being a need for a pesticide spraying campaign.

When it comes to getting rid of sins, virtues are a little bit like the birds. They gobble up sins. A man may not stop his drinking because of prohibition; he may, however, stop because of his love for his wife and family. Lying and stealing cannot exist with honesty; trickery and double-dealing cannot exist with faithfulness; greed cannot exist with open-handed charity.

In the Christian life, the accent is on the positive. St Paul tells us to fill our minds with "those things that are good and deserve praise: things that are true, noble, right, pure, lovely, and honourable" (Phil 4:8). We are not told any more what we may not do. We are told to go the second mile, to love our neighbour as ourselves, to forgive unto seventy times seven. When we think in these terms, murder and lying and stealing don't even enter the picture.

The Christian soldier takes life on the offensive. There is no retreat, no holding back, no standing still. Do you have an enemy? Don't just put up with him — pray for him! Love him, call down every kind of blessing around his head. God's wisdom lies in that command.

A friend of mine had her mother visiting on what turned out to be a more permanent basis than she had expected. The older woman was full of criticism, as elderly mothers sometimes are, and my friend was hard put to keep an even temper. She admitted that she had prayed for help but without much success. I asked her *how* she prayed for her mother, and the answer came back as quick as a flash.

"Oh, I don't pray for her. I pray for myself, that I may have more patience and love and kindness and generosity and . . ."

Now it has been my experience that if you pray for virtues like patience and love and kindness and generosity, what you will get is not a gentle stiffening of the moral fiber but the experience of someone crossing your path and demanding all the patience, love, kindness, and generosity you've got. Looked at from that point of view, my friend had already had her prayers answered in full.

Birds will not come to a bug-free garden. There's nothing to eat! In the same way, virtues will not grow in us if there's nothing for them to fight. Fortunately, we don't need to worry about that problem. All of us need to grow in virtue of one kind or another, and praying for virtues is like setting out birdbaths and feeding stations in your garden. We ought to give the invitation.

Going back to my friend, I still maintain that she should have been praying for her mother. By the time she was ready to pray for more patience and love, God had already answered that prayer. She needed to use what she had so that it could grow. What better way is there to show love for someone than to pray for him? It is almost impossible to be impatient, unloving or unkind to a person if only a short while before we have been on our knees begging God to give him his grace and favor.

The birds that nest in our trees do not wait with their beaks open for bugs to fall into their gullets. They go out and hunt them down. They dig under bark, dive-bomb the grass, and constantly keep a beady eye cocked for an unwary fly.

Similarly, if the virtues we have are going to grow, they must be militant and offensive. They need to be trained and drilled and stretched to the limit. It's no trick of the tongue that talks about *exercising* patience, *exercising* humility, *exercising* restraint. We don't talk about exercising joy or peace because we don't have to. When joy comes, it bubbles; when peace comes, it flows. But joy and peace are not virtues. They are the fruit of the Spirit, and these other virtues, like the birds, are their defenders.

It is "sweet, sweet, sweet poison" to feel able to imply "thus saith the Lord" at the end of every expression of our pet aversions.

C.S. Lewis

Our Lord found great significance in the life of birds; in their freedom, their self-abandoned trust, their release from mere carefulness. He held them precious to God, and patterns for the faith and hope of man.

Evelyn Underhill

Like birds hovering, so the Lord will protect Jerusalem;
He will protect and deliver it, he will spare and rescue it.

Isaiah 31:5

Teach me, O God, so to use all the circumstances of my life today that they may bring forth in me the fruits of holiness rather than the fruits of sin.
Let me use disappointment as material for patience:
Let me use success as material for thankfulness:
Let me use suspense as material for perseverance:
Let me use danger as material for courage:
Let me use reproach as material for longsuffering:
Let me use praises as material for humility:
Let me use pleasures as material for temperance:
Let me use pains as material for endurance.

John Baillie

Weeds

The garden chore I dislike more than anything else is weeding. It is back-breaking, time-consuming work that never seems to come to an end. Pull out a weed one day and its cousin will be there the next, greedily hogging all the light, moisture, and nourishing soil it can get. Weeds may be kept under control, but weeding never comes to an end.

There's a popular saying that a weed is only a flower in the wrong place. That's sentimental poppycock. With apologies to Gertrude Stein, a weed is a weed is a weed! A petunia in an onion patch would still be a petunia, and tomatoes growing in a rose bed would still be tomatoes. You might not want tomatoes in your rose bed, and you probably would pull them out if they happened to grow there, but you wouldn't say they were just weeds.

Weeds have a number of distinctive characteristics which mark them out from the desirable plants we normally cultivate in a garden. The first and most important distinction is that a weed normally isn't good for anything. It isn't particularly good to eat, and it produces neither edible fruit nor attractive flowers. There isn't a good reason for a gardener to give a weed growing room — and that's why it's a weed.

A second characteristic of weeds is that they grow without much encouragement. Given a little tolerance, they will spread across the neat furrows of a vegetable garden until they take over. Weeds don't waste energy putting out fruit and blossom.

They're in that garden for themselves, and every bit of sustenance they get goes to strengthening their own root, stem, and leaf structure. Weeds spread by producing some of the most tenacious seeds in the botanical kingdom, and sometimes they spread by underground runners. These little roots fan out under the soil and suddenly pop up in another location to grow a second plant, and a third, and so on. The result of this strong resilient growth is that the more delicate plants are choked out and smothered by plants that have no use at all.

The third characteristic of weeds is a direct result of the way they grow. Weeds are very hard to control. They won't stay in neatly defined boundaries. If you plant a seed of corn, it comes up where you plant it and produces its fruit. Corn won't insist on sending a runner underground to sprout up among the string beans. If weeds were people, you might say they were disobedient!

Sometimes there is a very fine dividing line between weeds and cultivated plants. The dandelion, for instance, can be useful. Its bright, yellow flower is pretty to look at, and if you collect enough of them, the blossoms can be used to make dandelion wine. The leaves make excellent salad greens, and the roots when roasted and ground make a fine caffeine-free substitute for coffee! With so many points in its favour, you would think that everyone would be out there growing dandelions. But who would dare? We get enough dandelions in the grass and flower-beds without asking for more. Overnight those cheerful little blossoms turn to white puffballs that blow away with the first breeze, spreading thousands of seeds wherever the wind blows. A row of dandelions planted in my vegetable garden would yield a crop of nothing but dandelions by the summer's end. Although this weed has the possibility of being quite a useful plant, dandelion salad is a luxury most gardeners choose to forego.

Snow-on-the-mountain is a plant that just squeaks into the flower category. I had some in my rock garden once — an attractive plant with lovely white blossoms in early summer, and a gray-green foliage the rest of the time. But it spread. I seemed to spend more time trying to keep that planting under control than I did on anything else in my garden. It grew into the roots of my dwarf pines, and I scratched my fingers trying to pull it out. It began to come up through the pink blossom of the thyme, and wind itself around the roots of the baby iris. Finally, in utter frustration, I tore every bit of the plant out. Attractive though it was, snow-on-the-mountain wasn't worth all the trouble it caused me. It was too much like a weed.

Spiritually, some people are a lot like weeds, and most of us have at least some tendency in that direction. Weeds don't do anybody any good, and the same thing is often true of people. They live their own lives without any care or concern for the welfare of others. They make a good salary but give nothing to the work of the church or the poor. Their leisure time is spent in self-centred activities that afford only personal pleasure. The claims of the community, and even family responsibilities, are shrugged off in the headlong pursuit of self-fulfillment and self-enrichment.

Weeds spread and, unfortunately, so do human weeds. We all have the opportunity in this life to be an influence for good or for ill. The man or woman who spends his life getting and spending is setting an example that someone else will follow. We all know what it means to keep up with the Joneses, and most of us have been guilty of it at some point in our lives. But if someone is going to keep up with us, what do we want to see copied? The expensive new car that sits in our driveway, or our concern for underprivileged youth shown through involvement in the big brother movement or guiding or some similar organization?

Weeds are very hard to control, and of course that is the major problem with human weeds. We all want to have things our own way and to grow in our own broad spaces. It's a good and natural instinct, within reason, but there have to be limits for all of us. One person's freedom ends where the rights of the next person begin. God has plans for each one of us, just as the gardener has plans for the flowers in his garden, but we must be obedient for these plans to be fulfilled. It is illuminating to see how many of the Ten Commandments have to do with this very problem of growing into another flower-bed and choking out the growth in it. *You shall not kill. You shall not commit adultery. You shall not steal. You shall not bear false witness against your neighbour. You shall not covet your neighbour's house, or his wife, or his manservant, or his ox, or his ass or anything that is your neighbour's.* Obedience to these laws forms the bare minimum requirement to keep us from weedlike growth.

Someone once told me that the only real sin is saying no to God. It's a very profound thought, and moving in its simplicity. But in order for us to know when we are saying no to God, we must first of all understand what he requires of us. The Ten Commandments are a beginning, but Jesus took us far beyond them when he told us to love our enemies and to do good to them that hate us. The person who can do this is in no danger of being a weed!

An important point to keep in mind is that all flowers, vegetables, and other useful plants were once wild. They grew in the fields and forests with those self-same weeds we despise today. And then someone found a use for them, brought them into the garden, and cultivated them. Seeds were cross-pollinated, and more desirable strains were developed — sweeter corn, juicier tomatoes, more fragrant roses, brighter zinnias. Gardeners and botanists have worked on these plants over the centuries, and particularly in our own time now that the laws of genetics are better understood. Thanks to that labour, we are able to enjoy a bewildering array of flowers and vegetables that were almost totally unknown to our ancestors.

In the same way, God still works on the weeds in the field outside the garden of his church. Let a weed produce ever so slight a blossom, or the tiniest of edible fruits, and the master gardener of all time is there to encourage such growth and to help the plant develop to its full potential. The smallest of kind actions is a movement toward God, especially when it is done by a person who is not in the habit of being kind.

Jesus said that God makes his sun rise on the evil and on the good, and sends rain on the just and the unjust (Matt 5:45). The weeds in the field and the flowers in the garden live through the same storms and the same heat of day. But the flowers in the garden are cared for by the gardener. They are picked and pruned and trimmed. The ground around their roots is carefully cultivated so that the slightest rainfall will be absorbed, while the weeds in the field receive no benefit from the same rain because the ground around their roots has baked hard in the sun, and the rain evaporates before it can penetrate the earth.

It's a tough world outside the garden, and the weeds know it. They don't have time to grow fruit and flowers. They're living in a jungle, and the best they can do is to survive. Sometimes people say the same thing about being a Christian. It's a tough world out there, they say. It's a jungle, and you can't take time to worry about the other guy.

The difference is that Christians never live in a jungle. No matter where we go, the gardener goes with us. In fact, he goes before us, preparing the ground. The jungle may teem around us, but wherever we are, there should be a little patch of ordered beauty. And because the gardener is there, we are tended and cared for in ways beyond our imagining. The drop of grace that would be lost on unprepared ground becomes the moisture on which our roots feed and draw strength in difficult circumstances. We are never left entirely to our own will, never allowed to grow wild, and never left defenceless against encroaching weeds and insects. We may be pruned and we may be trimmed, but we are never left untended.

Of course, the analogy can only go so far. Weeds appear to be useless, but probably if a botanist spent enough time and effort, he could find a use for many of them. People aren't weeds, however, and God made each one of us for a definite purpose. If we become useless, it is because of our sin. Obedience to God's will for our lives is the only requirement for entry into his garden. We cannot plant ourselves, like stray seeds blown in on the wind. We have to be planted by his hand and be obedient to it.

I asked the Great Creator what the universe was made for.

"Ask for something more in keeping with that little mind of yours," He replied.

"What was man made for?"

"Little man, you still want to know too much. Cut down the extent of your request and improve the intent."

Then I told the Creator I wanted to know all about the peanut. He replied that my mind was too small to know all about the peanut, but He said he would give me a handful of peanuts. And God said, "Behold I have given you every herb bearing seed, which is upon the face of the earth . . . to you it shall be for meat . . . I have given every green herb for meat: and it was so."

I carried the peanuts into my laboratory and the Creator told me to take them apart and resolve them into their elements. With such knowledge as I had of chemistry and physics I set to work to take them apart. I separated the water, the fats, the oils, the gums, the resins, sugars, starches, pectoses, pentosans, amino acids. There! I had the parts of the peanuts all spread out before me.

I looked at him and he looked at me. "Now you know what the peanut is."

"Why did you make the peanut?"

The Creator said, "I have given you three laws; namely, compatibility, temperature, and pressure. All you have to do is take these constituents and put them together, observing these laws, and I will show you why I made the peanut."

George Washington Carver

(Carver went on to develop over 300 uses for the peanut, including peanut butter and oil.)

Then the disciples came and said to him, "Do you know that the Pharisees were offended when they heard this saying?" He answered, "Every plant which my heavenly Father has not planted will be rooted up."

Matthew 15:12, 13

Indoor Gardening

No book about gardening would be really complete without a section on house plants. The indoor garden set in a sunny window can be the making of an otherwise unattractive room. With interior decoration in mind, I have always had an ambition to have some such display of green and flowering foliage. The trouble is you have to start small, and I never seem to be able to keep more than one or two plants on the go at a time. I keep falling into the same traps over and over again.

One of my problems is watering too much (unless I forget altogether). When a new plant appears on the scene I find myself hovering over it solicitously, wondering whether at last this will be the one to make the grade and survive. The giver, or else the clerk in the store, has told me to water the plant once a week. But how much water? I fill it once to the brim of the pot, and because this is soaked up quickly, I take pity on the poor thing, knowing that it won't have another drink for a whole week, and fill it up again. Or else I water on Tuesdays and passing by on Friday, I notice the earth in the pot is bone dry. Perhaps, I think with remorse, I didn't put enough in! So out with the watering can.

It doesn't really matter how it happens. What matters is that the plant is sitting up to its neck in slush for the better part of the week. And while it looks good and healthy and beautifully watered for a start, there comes a point when the leaves turn yellow and the plant droops over and the roots are rotted underneath it. I ruined two African violets this way before someone told me what was happening.

Now water should be good for plants, and outdoors we seldom think of plants getting too much water. This is because there is a natural form of drainage built into most gardens. Where there is poor drainage, plants will not thrive at all. What we see in the overwatered house plant is essentially what we find in a piece of higher ground suddenly become swampy because of some damming project. The trees and bushes are unable to cope with the vast amounts of water and inevitably die as their roots rot like the house plants'.

This can happen to us too. We get a spiritual watering through the grace of God, and it leaves us feeling green and lush and good. And since we like feeling this way, it's only natural that we should hope to get watered fairly often. But God knows what is best for us, and if we are patient about it, we won't get watered more than once a week (or its spiritual equivalent!). This may be uncomfortable, but it does keep us healthy. We have to realize that we are not really all that good or virtuous, and so we learn humility in our prayers.

There are people who have a strong religious experience, a watering, and who go looking for more of the same. And if they are very persistent about it, God does not always seem to say No to them. And if he grants the request in even a little degree, they are able to magnify it with emotional fervor. When it comes in this way, religious experience never feels the same or as good, but they still go on asking.

People who treat God in this way, who look for the gifts and not the Giver, are in the same boat with my house plants. Their roots are rotting under them. A great French bishop once wrote: "There are many souls who experience these tendernesses and consolations, and who, nevertheless, are very vicious, and consequently, have not a true love of God, much less true devotion."

The second problem I have had with house plants concerned their pots. I've never learned to repot a plant successfully, and so I always tend to avoid the job until it's too late and the plant is hopelessly rootbound. It's a pitiful sight to take such a plant out of a pot and find its roots all tangled and tied up inside each other, with the whole lump of earth encased in a webbed mass of white roots. House plants, as they grow in size, are supposed to be transplanted into bigger pots so that their roots will have something to grow into.

The newest thing in growing seedlings is peat pots — little pots made out of peat moss. The idea is that as the plants grow, their roots will be able to grow right through the pot, and then when they are ready to be planted outside, they can be put straight into the ground, pot and all, with no transplanting shock to the roots. It ought to work very well, and in most cases it does. But a few years ago, I bought a young cedar tree in a peat pot from a nursery that specializes in that kind of thing, and for some reason the roots didn't grow through. At the critical point when the roots reached the pot, they were turned aside, unable to penetrate and grow through it.

At first the little tree seemed to be getting along well enough, even though it wasn't growing very fast. Then gradually it began to get straggly and thin-foliaged. I dug it up and there was the pot, hard and unyielding, and inside was a mess of white roots. Fortunately it wasn't too late, and the tree once freed from its prison took a new lease on life.

I think sometimes we get rootbound by things that were meant to help us in the beginning. There are ideas about God that are helpful to a child but not to an adult; there are prayers suitable for the beginner but not for the more mature Christian. The new convert may cling to his first teacher instead of learning to depend on God, or he may stay utterly within the confines of the first Christian community to which he was drawn (be it prayer group, Bible study, or congregation). All of these experiences that come to us are things that we are meant to grow through. We do not cast them aside or throw them away. We go through them as the plant grows through the peat pot, penetrating and passing through it at every point, so that it becomes part of the very fabric of its existence.

In the Christian life, we can never say that we have arrived.

We are always on the way. If there comes a point when we find a congenial circle, a place where we are satisfied and wish to stay, then we stop reaching out in our search for God. Like the plant, we too can become rootbound in a pot of our own making, a pot of narrow conviction and prejudice. When Jesus blamed the Pharisees, it was for this very narrowness of spirit. They were so utterly rootbound by their attention to the detail of the law that they could not recognize the larger scope of the garden beyond.

Now all this does not mean that there are no barriers, no bounds, no outer limits at all. A garden after all has boundaries, and it may have a fence. But a fence is not a pot! A fence is meant to keep marauders out; a pot is meant to keep a plant in. There is a world of difference. As long as we are in the larger garden of the church, we will have all the openness and freedom we need to grow to our full stature as children of God. The openness of the garden does not mean that we will not be set in a particular flower bed, or if you like, in a particular denomination of the church. It does mean, however, that we ought to be mortally careful of how we castigate our fellow Christians, or by what prejudice and party loyalty we allow ourselves to be bound.

Somehow we seem to have slipped from the subject of indoor gardening back to the great outdoors. After all, house plants are only outdoor plants, brought into the house to live under artificial conditions. They are given warmth and heat and light in complete disregard of nature. While all else lies in frozen calm, you can have narcissus and tulips blooming in your window.

Normally God does not seem to care for hothouse plants, but there have been times in the history of the church when everything lay in a kind of frozen wilderness and one or two people bloomed out of season, so to speak, forcing the church to return to its first Lord and Master. The Old Testament talks about God raising up his prophets, and so God raises up certain people, giving them grace in special ways to withstand the temper of their times.

We must realize that these consolations will not last forever, and we must humbly beg of God the grace to serve him in dryness of soul, when it will so please him. In the meantime, instead of trying to prolong these consolations by our own mental efforts, we must moderate them and cling steadfastly to the God of all consolations.

A. Tanqueray

There are times when God may suggest very quietly some duty, or action, that he desires us to do; but we are not on the alert, and the thought scarcely stirs a ripple on the surface of our mind. Only later do we find out that we have let someone down, or forgotten some urgent duty. To live in this careless way causes prayer to droop and wilt, like houseplants in a stuffy room.

Olive Wyon

As she lay dying, a flowering twig of wild pear-blossom had been brought into her sick-room from a tree which had unexpectedly flowered when all else on the hill-side was parched and dry. She glowed over the surprise of it, and caressed it with artist's hands, saying with intense delight: "Oh, that's so like souls: you never know when they'll break out."

Life of Lilias Trotter

The Growing Time

Most really enthusiastic gardeners tend to while away the long winter evenings by curling up in front of the fireplace with their garden books and seed catalogues. Planning what they will plant in the coming spring keeps them busy for hours.

For the expert as well as the novice planner, one of the most useful sections in a garden book is the part with charts and diagrams that tell when certain flowers bloom or how long they take to grow from seed. It seems you never know enough about this. Lilacs and tulips usually bloom about the same time, but if you plant early tulips and late lilacs, they may miss each other completely! And you won't have any pretty bouquets either. Of course, lilacs and tulips are a breeze if you know what you're doing. The expert gardener goes on to more complicated combinations, aided like the beginner with his blooming timetable.

Sometimes in the Christian life, we think it would be very helpful if we had a chart to go by, something to tell us what we can expect in the way of self-improvement within a given period. We set ourselves up in a program of prayer and good works, and console ourselves with the thought that if we only stick with it for six months (or even six weeks!), we will have conquered this failing or acquired that virtue. We think this way because we set up goals for ourselves, something to strive for. We want an orderly progression of improvement in ourselves, and being human, we want to see it happen.

It is helpful and necessary to have goals if we are going to grow. We need to get pointed in the right direction just as the tulip bulb needs to be planted with the growing side up. The difference is that the tulip is not bothered about when it will bloom. Late or early, it responds just as fast as it can to the warmth and moisture of the spring earth, and in due time, according to the gardener's timetable, it reaches out from the earth into the bright sunshine and blooms. The tulip neither knows nor cares about the particular time of its blooming; it simply acts according to its particular nature. It is the gardener who has the job of knowing when it will bloom.

Very often we forget that God's time is not our time. He knows our nature better than we do ourselves; he knows what we can do, and he knows our ultimate possibilities. We do not need to set time limits or be impatient with ourselves about our failures. If we only continue to respond to him in the best way we can, God is not impatient with our slowness any more than a gardener is impatient with a late tulip.

Patience is one of the peculiar Christian virtues. It is seldom mentioned in the Old Testament writings, but in the gospels and epistles of the New Testament it comes into full focus. We are told to work patiently and to wait patiently and above all to *be* patient. There is a strong sense that God is at work in the world and that nothing can thwart the designs of his all-embracing love if we are only faithful and patient.

There are two kinds of waiting, as everyone knows. One is fretful and fussy, with an eye on the clock and a nagging fear that the expected event may not happen in time; and the other kind of waiting is peaceful and calm, neither hurried nor worried, without any fear of passing time because the end result is assured. The gardener does not worry because the late tulips don't bloom with the early ones. He knows that their time will come. Similarly, we can be sure that once we have put our lives wholeheartedly into the hands of God, we do not need to worry about our progress. We still need to work at our growing and to respond to his call, now more than ever, but we do not need to be cross and impatient with ourselves because of our slowness. St Paul writing to the Philippians said he was sure "that God, who began this good work in you, will carry it on until it is finished in the Day of Christ Jesus" (Phil 1:6).

It is this trust in God's action that makes us patient. We have a sure hope in the future. We don't need to see the chart of our development any more than the flowers do. Not knowing the rate of our growth has the added advantage of keeping us humble. We may go on for years, stumbling over the same faults and never seeming to make any progress in spite of our most earnest efforts. Others are shooting past us, laying hold of all kinds of goodness and virtue, and to all appearances, finding it remarkably easy. We wonder what's wrong with us.

The chances are that nothing is wrong with us, if we are still trying. The man who plants a bush doesn't expect or want it to grow as tall as his trees, and he will probably keep trimming it at the top so that it bushes out at the bottom. If he plants an oak tree, he won't expect it to grow as fast as his neighbour's locust, and he is content to wait because he wants an oak. In the same way, God is quite content for us to grow according to our nature. He does not expect us to be like anyone else. He wants us to be ourselves, as he created us, to the best of our ability.

We all know that growing is not a thing of effort, but is the result of an inward life-principle of growth. All the stretching and pulling in the world could not make a dead oak grow; but a live oak grows without stretching. It is plain, therefore, that the essential thing is to get within you the growing life, and then you cannot help but grow. And this life is the "life hid with Christ in God," the wonderful divine life of an indwelling Holy Ghost. . . . Put your growing into his hands as completely as you have put all your other affairs. Suffer him to manage it as he will. Do not concern yourself about it, nor even think of it.

Hannah Whitall Smith

God is teaching you to trust him implicitly and not to rely on yourself and your own efforts. . . . Just carry on, don't try to estimate whether things are improving or not. We are the worst possible judges about that ourselves. There is often a temptation to pull up the plant and see how it is getting on. But roots grow in the dark and unseen and unknown and when they are strong the flower blossoms and the fruit comes into being.

Raymond Raynes

Be patient, then, my brothers, until the Lord comes. See how the farmer is patient as he waits for his land to produce precious crops. He waits patiently for the autumn and spring rains. And you also must be patient! Keep your hopes high, for the day of the Lord's coming is near.

James 5:7,8

The First Frost

The first morning of the fall, when the fine white hoar frost appears on the ground, is a time for sadness. The plants will not survive much longer. The perennials, the bushes, and the trees will soon have dropped their leaves and gone into the dormant state of winter, waiting for the warm sun and rush of spring water to revive them.

It has been said that the very fact of winter and summer, of cold death and warm life springing up again, should speak to us of resurrection and a life after death. I am sure that God does speak to us through the world he has made, if we only had ears to hear. Jesus spoke constantly to his disciples in parables, perhaps to show that the simple incidents of our daily lives have a deeper meaning than we think, but certainly to put spiritual truth into understandable terms.

But parables are only parables. They tell truth but do not tie up all the loose ends. I cannot, for instance, think why there should be both annual and perennial plants, or what meaning it has for us, unless it has something to say about the doctrine of eternal life as opposed to the uncomfortable thought of final and irrevocable death.

The best gardeners I know are sold on perennials, and the object of every good gardener's planning is to have one "ever-blooming border" composed completely of perennials.

Annuals bloom right through the summer, and for the new garden, or for the inexperienced gardener like myself, they

provide a delightful show of color. But it is perennials that ulti-
mately form the backbone of the flower bed. With the excep-
tion of a few plants like roses, perennials bloom only once
during the summer and then retire into the background. The
job of the gardener is to know whether they bloom in July or
August. Then by combining them in a planting with other
perennials that bloom at different seasons, he can be sure of
having a constant display of color from early spring to
autumn. It is not necessary or even desirable for everything to
bloom all the time, but as the season changes, first one plant
and then another will come into focus.

From an amateur point of view, the best thing about perennials is that you can count on them! Given reasonable care,
they will come up year after year, growing ever larger and
stronger with the passage of time. Like annuals, they can be
grown from seed, but it is a chancy business. They can be
spread through the garden much more easily and surely by the
simple process of dividing the roots. Certainly given a choice, I
would rather grow lilies from bulbs than from seed.

Now in God's garden — the church — there are people who
count as perennials and there are others who are annuals. The
perennials are the ones who stick with it even when the going is
rough, when other people get the spotlight, and some of their
old blooms and foliage are cut back in order to make room for
somebody else's blooming period. They don't give up, and
their time comes again. But the annuals expect to be on show
all the time, rather like the Pharisees that Jesus talked about,
who fasted and tithed and stood about in the market place with
long fringes on their shawls, trying to look holy.

The end result with the annuals, of course, is that they can't
keep up the pace. Flowers that expend all their energy in
blooming have no foliage left to build up the big tuberous roots
of the perennial plant. Come the frost, they die. Fortunately,
they can grow again from seed, but they are not as certain to
come up again in the spring as plants grown from a perennial
root.

There is nothing intrinsically good about a perennial. After all, there are perennial weeds too! Their main virtue lies in their dependability, tenacity, and if you like, faithfulness. Annuals, on the other hand, seem to thrive in a garden chiefly because this is the one place where they are not troubled with weeds and grass. Most perennials will continue to come up for at least a few years in an overgrown garden. But not annuals! They can't take it because they haven't got the necessary root to hold their own nourishment and to fight off the weeds.

For the same reason, we find so many "annuals" in the church. Here is the climate of love and understanding that nourishes them as young seedlings — here they are able to reach into the love of God because they are in a cultivated flower bed. In the beginning there is no obvious difference between the annual and perennial seedlings. Then the annuals start to bloom!

Young perennial flowers, grown from seed, will often have no bloom at all for several seasons until they have built up a good strong root. But the annuals bloom right away. As Christians, they walk around spreading sweetness and light, and they never seem to have any spiritual difficulties at all. Too often, the perennials are fooled into thinking that this is for real. The peony wonders if it will ever bloom again when the chrysanthemum finally comes into flower, and they both look around in amazement at the petunias . . . until winter comes.

There are people who are converted and bloom like crazy. They run around trying to convert everyone else, but never take time or trouble to become more deeply converted themselves, to grow big roots into the love of God. Like the annuals, they think that blooming or "witnessing" is all that matters. Their roots are fine and shallow, and they depend too much upon the freshness of their experience of God. When a drought comes, a time of testing in prayer, they wilt visibly. Come the black frost, they die.

We are not plants. We are people — rational and spiritual human beings made in the image of God and called to be his children. Unlike the plants, we have the opportunity of choosing what we will be — annual or perennial. If we live as annuals, there will always be the danger that we will not be able to reseed ourselves, that a second or third conversion may not "take," and we will never grow and spread out in the manner of the mature perennial.

In our lives we will meet with many frosts before the killing one, many winters before the final one, and many springs before the eternal one. This is the trying and the testing ground, the time of our opportunity and our judgment.

> *"Good morning," said the little prince.*
> *"Good morning," said the flower.*
> *"Where are the men?" the little prince asked, politely.*
> *The flower had once seen a caravan passing.*
> *"Men?" she echoed. "I think there are six or seven of them in existence. I saw them, several years ago. But one never knows where to find them. The wind blows them away. They have no roots, and that makes their life very difficult."*
> Antoine de Saint Exupéry

Since you have accepted Christ Jesus as Lord, live in union with him. Keep your roots deep in him, build your lives on him, and become ever stronger in your faith, as you were taught. And be filled with thanksgiving.
Colossians 2:6,7

The Promise of Spring

When the air is filled with the smell of burning leaves and the trees poke their bare branches into the sky, we know that the heavy blanket of winter is just around the corner. Yet no matter how cold the wind or deep the snow, we are left with the assurance that spring will come. Early or late, when it will come we do not know. But it will come.

Scrape the bark of a dormant tree and the trunk underneath it is green and fresh. The buds for the coming spring have been formed before the dead leaves of autumn have even fallen to the ground.

Jesus Christ is our promise of a spring to come. He is the Resurrection and the Life. No matter how terrifying the thought of death may be, we are reassured if we place our hope in him.

But there are smaller winters in our lives too — those "winters of discontent" that chill the soul and numb the heart. We are frozen by fears and uncertainties that we have no right to entertain, and being frozen we are unable to respond to those things that we know we ought to do.

The dormant tree is a "sleeping" tree. Dormant is the French word for "sleeping." The tree is not dead but sleeping. "The child is not dead but sleeping" (Luke 8:52). Our Lord who raised the dead to life is quite capable of raising us from whatever frozen state of sorrow or sin we happen to be in.

The answer for us is the same as for the tree. We need to be in the sun — the warm, spring sun — which will melt all the ice and frost away. Jesus is our Sun, the Light of the World. If we put ourselves in his presence *even without doing anything else*, he will have an effect on us. Sit in the sun for an hour and you will have the beginning of a tan (or perhaps a sunburn). You did not have to do anything to get a tan. You simply had to expose yourself to the sun.

Exposing ourselves to God as the sunbather exposes bare flesh to the sun is the basic secret. We have to leave ourselves open to him, not hiding our faults or making excuses or finding any other reason for covering up. Sometimes this process hurts a bit — not us, but our pride and sensibilities and self-esteem. But in the end it can do us nothing but good. Confession before God and utter honesty about all our failings and distress is the only way to get on the sunny side of the street.

It is the sunny side of the street that always thaws first in the springtime. The crocuses come up there first, and then the tulips. The grass is green and growing while there are still banks of dirty ice across the way. Spring comes each year and fulfills its promise of the year before. Those bare branches burst into bloom and thick greenery. The birds return and winter seems a long time ago. In the end, we have a sure hope of an eternal spring, of an eternal life. And in the meantime, God has not left us comfortless.

St Paul writes that the Holy Spirit is the guarantee of all that God has in store for us (2 Cor 1:22). We have the Spirit as the first of God's gifts. And so springtime should begin right now in our day-to-day lives. The New Testament is full of allusions to the new life that we have in Jesus Christ. Hearts and minds must be made completely new (Eph 4:23). This is the work of the Holy Spirit, and as the flower in the spring puts out new shoots and unfolds fresh blossoms to the sun, so we too will be renewed as we turn to God and wait for him.

The first time I saw Brother Lawrence was upon the 3rd of August, 1666. He told me that God had done him a singular favour in his conversion at the age of eighteen. That in the winter, seeing a tree stripped of its leaves, and considering that within a little time the leaves would be renewed and after that the flowers and fruit appear, he received a high view of the providence and power of God, which has never since been effaced from his soul. That this view had perfectly set him loose from the world, and kindled in him such a love for God that he could not tell whether it had increased during the more than forty years he had lived since.

Brother Lawrence's Biographer

We give thee thanks for the loveliness of spring with its promise of summer.

Bird and blossom seem to tell us of the possibility of new life for our own souls. This spring day speaks to us of beginning again, of new beauty that can come to refurbish our own barren lives.

O Lord Jesus, may that transformation begin in us now as we sit before thee — penitent and expectant. Amen.

Peter Marshall

The City

For people who live in the city, gardens are sometimes the only point of contact with that vital world of nature beyond their immediate circle of brick and asphalt. No matter how limited his resources, the dedicated gardener will find a way to produce — something. On a visit to Rome, I was astonished by the flowers and lush greenery on the balconies of all the apartment buildings. Window boxes, plastic containers, tin cans had all been put into service to grow everything from geraniums and tomatoes to orange trees! With light and only limited space, gardens had been created from almost nothing.

Living in the midst of a busy, noisy city with the constant hum of traffic, the whines and growls and bangs of heavy trucks and busses and construction equipment, the pervasive smell of exhaust fumes and the gritty dust that settles on everything — living in the midst of all this, I sometimes longed for the country. The tiny spot of thin grass that was ours provided some relief, but I longed to be away from the noise and congestion and the problems of city life. I thought of shaded, leafy woods and wildflowers growing untended by the thousands, of calm lakes in the evening and the cry of wild geese settling down for the night, of meadows covered in buttercups with blue mountain peaks in the distance, of tall, dark pine trees standing in rocky ravines with fast-running streams. No one tends or gardens all this beauty. It is simply there to be enjoyed.

Nature is a puzzle to us. On the one hand we look at the inherent beauty of the natural world and we are tempted to believe in the myth of Mother Nature beneficiently bestowing her gifts of plenty on those who cooperate in her grand designs. Somehow, we can't help thinking, if only we could all go back to the simpler, purer life of the countryside, then we could really live "the good life" in harmony with nature. Throughout the history of civilization, people have longed to escape from the cities for just that purpose. Sometimes it has even become fashionable. In the court of Marie Antoinette, ladies-in-waiting dressed up as dairymaids and pretended to milk cows. The French philosopher Rousseau had popularized the idea of the Noble Savage, untouched by evil, and hundreds of migrants went to the New World hoping to shake themselves free of the corruption and vice in the societies they knew. In our own day, we have seen the same longing for purity and the same flight from the cities into small, rural communities. The demand for natural foods, natural fibres, and folk medicines is based at least partly on the assumption that natural is always better than synthetic, that natural is somehow *good*.

The other side of nature is the nasty side, the side where we don't see a mother at all. The poet Tennyson talked about "nature, red in tooth and claw," and there is nothing gentle about a wolf hunting down a rabbit for its dinner. The beautiful mountain peak may turn into a seething volcano, belching floods of molten lava and poisonous gases over miles of countryside. The trickling stream in the pine forest may suddenly become a fierce torrent of water in spring flood, ripping up everything that stands in its path. The farmer may get so much rain that all his potatoes rot in the ground, or so little that the corn simply dries up on the withered stalks. At times like this, we don't think nature is particularly good.

The Bible tells us that when God first created the earth, he looked at what he had done and saw that it was very good. Nevertheless, in the good world that he had created, God planted a garden and there he put the man whom he had formed. The man was supposed to till the garden and take care of it. Of course, everyone knows the sad story of what followed — how the man and the woman disobeyed God and ate the fruit of the tree which they were not to touch, and how they were turned out of the garden into the wilderness to work soil which was inhospitable and thorny.

God planted a garden. In the midst of the natural wilderness of an unfallen world, God created a place of beauty and order where the man he had formed could work and find nurture. When the man and his wife were turned out of the garden, their natural instinct was to try to recreate the beauty and order they had known in Eden. We have been trying to do this ever since, but we can never go back to that garden. At the beginning of the Bible we read about the garden. At the end of the Bible we read about the city, and the garden and the city are tied together in a remarkable way. The planting of that garden marked the very beginning of civilization — the taming of the wilderness. The coming down of the heavenly city, the New Jerusalem, will mark the end of that journey, for here is the true taming of the wilderness in the hearts of men and women. Our innocence is lost. We cannot go back to the garden; we must go forward to the city.

The City of God is different from any city we have ever known, just as the Garden of Eden was different from any garden we have ever tried to plant. In the Revelation of St John, there are attempts to describe it, but how can we really imagine what he is trying to tell us? The streets are of gold, but the gold is transparent as glass! The city gates are each made of an enormous pearl. And if you want to think about urban sprawl, the city is 1,400 miles long and wide and high!

A river flowed through the Garden of Eden to water it, and in *Revelation* we read that a river bearing the water of life flows through the middle of the City of God. It flows from the throne of God down the middle of the great street of the city, and the water is as clear as crystal. On each side of the river stands the tree of life, whose leaves are for the healing of the nations. No longer will there be a curse, says St John, and we remember that the tree of life stood in the Garden of Eden. It was for that reason that God turned Adam and Eve out of the garden, for he did not want them to eat of the tree of life and live forever in their sin. We cannot go back to the Garden because it doesn't exist anymore. It has become the City.

The thought of spending eternal life in a city is not an appealing one, especially when we think of the dirt and crime and crowded housing of our own cities. In fact, when C.S. Lewis wanted to find an image of Hell for his book *The Great Divorce*, he described a grimy mill-town with run-down houses. It was not a place of fiery torment, but a dreary city filled with self-centred people living their own little lives in their own little houses with dirty lace curtains at the windows. It is hard to think of heaven being that kind of city. St John gives an image of another city, an earthly city whose "sins are piled up to heaven" — Babylon the Great. As the New Jerusalem is the pure and holy Bride of Christ, so Babylon is the great harlot who commits adultery with the kings of the earth, while the merchants of the earth grow rich from her excessive luxuries (Rev 18:35). We know about cities like that. We know about dirt and disease, inequalities and moral corruption. A retreat to the wilderness sometimes appears to be the only solution.

The problem is that in retreating to the wilderness, we take our own fallen nature with us, and it is our fallen nature that is the root cause of all our problems. Send ten selfish people on a canoe trip in the Canadian north and they will probably create an instant slum as they leave a trail of litter wherever they go. The colonists who came to the New World, hoping to escape from the corruption of Europe, often found their very existence was threatened by the greed of some who came with them. Nature, although it is a good creation, is not good in the way that God is good. Nature has no power to redeem us.

In the city we have to deal with other people; in the wilderness we have to deal with ourselves. Perhaps that is an important first step everyone needs to take. We read of Moses, the Children of Israel, Elijah, John the Baptist, and even Jesus, being driven out into the wilderness to be tested. We all need an opportunity to get our priorities straight and to find the direction of our lives. Then we need to come back into the city to live with other people. Cities can be good places to live or they can be terrible places to live. Everything depends on who else lives there, on the laws that the city has, and whether the laws are observed. Are the streets safe at night? Are the poor adequately housed? Do the schools really offer an education? Are there parks and playgrounds? Do people paint their front doors and plant flowers? A city can only be as good as its citizens.

There is nothing innately bad about a city, except for the fallen nature of its inhabitants. Just as we have learned that the church is not a building but the people who worship in that building, so we have to understand that a city does not consist of buildings, but of the people who inhabit those buildings. The buildings may be beautiful, with all the modern conveniences, but the only thing that matters is whether the citizens have the will to form a good community. If they have that will, the most dilapidated, outmoded, run-down structures will not stop them. It was during the blitz in World War II that Londoners really came into their own as citizens of a great city. Thousands of people camped in subway stations while their homes were levelled to the ground by the enemy bombardment. People trusted each other, shared what they had, and strengthened each other through difficult days.

Unfortunately, it often takes hard times to bring out the best in people. In *Revelation*, St John writes about the times of tribulation that Christians will have to endure before the end comes. When that will be, we do not know. Jesus said, "No man knows the day or the hour," but he did tell us to look for the signs in the way we look for the weather. We live in a generation that is becoming increasingly concerned over the threat of a widespread nuclear holocaust. We know that the end could happen.

The comforting promise of God in this situation is that the end is not really the end. In fact, the end when it comes will be more in the nature of a beginning. Jesus will return in glory to rule his kingdom, and the New Jerusalem will descend from heaven. How can we talk sensibly about things which are beyond our understanding? The imagery is there to tell us truth, but we cannot expect to understand fully those things which are outside our experience. We can only hope to comprehend a little bit of the vision by analogy and by parable.

We have moved from the garden through the wilderness to the city. It is the journey of mankind, but it is also the journey that each must make in his own lifetime — born in innocence, tainted by sin, redeemed by God. Adam and Eve could not return to the Garden, for the way was barred by an angel with a flaming sword, but the twelve pearl gates of the New Jerusalem stand wide open to anyone who is ready to be washed and made clean. The gates of heaven are never closed.

And in some strange way, that city will be like a garden, for we are the plants under God's care and we have the blossoms and fruit that he wants to enjoy. On the other hand, we have no need of earth because we are rooted in God himself. We do not need rain because God is the living water that flows through the centre of the city. We do not need the sun because all light comes from the glory of God. The Garden of Eden has become the City of God, and — mystery of mysteries — that city is also a garden. We are the plants bearing blossom and fruit, cared for by the loving hand of the Gardener.

The heavenly vision is given to us that we may understand our destiny and not be afraid. It is also given to us so that we may understand the work we have to do now. The Bible tells us that here we have no abiding city (Heb 13:14). Our citizenship is in heaven (Phil 3:20), and we are fellow citizens with God's people everywhere (Eph 2:19). But that doesn't mean we can sit back and wait to enjoy life in the hereafter. The city is still being built — now, this minute — and the buildings of that city are people. The foundations were laid with the apostles and the prophets, with Jesus Christ as the chief cornerstone, but we are the bricks and stones of that city — living stones, just as Jesus is the living Stone (1 Pet 2:4). God is the builder (Heb 10:11) and God is the Gardener (John 15:1). We are the people of his planting and the garden of his delight.

Every saint in heaven is as a flower in the garden of God.
                                                        Jonathan Edwards

I think of my children asking me why God created mankind if mankind was going to make battlefields and slums and insane asylums. The city around our pleasant apartment building is not an easy place in which to see the hand of God. Mankind has imposed its imprint of ugly buildings and dirty buildings and desperate people. But if I cannot see God's love here on the Upper West Side of New York where we have done everything possible to destroy the beauty of creation, it is going to do me little good to rejoice in beauty in the uncluttered world of the country.

My breath steams the window but I see a young man walking along the street, his head bowed against the wind. It is cold, but for the moment the city is quiet. No sirens shrieking, no grinding of brakes. A light goes on in the window across the street.

It is the nature of love to create, and no matter what we do to creation, that love is still there, creating; in the young man who is holding his jacket closed across his chest; in you; in me.
                                                        Madeleine L'Engle

However dismal and catastrophic may be the present circumstances, we know we are not alone, for God dwells with us in life's most confining and oppressive cells. And even if we die there without having received the earthly promise, he shall lead us down that mysterious road called death, and at last to that indescribable city he has prepared for us. His creative power is not exhausted by this earthly life, nor is his majestic love locked within the limited walls of time and space.
                                                        Martin Luther King

Acknowledgments

Down to Earth
The Oxford Book of English Verse. London and New York: Oxford University Press, 1927; #793, by Thomas Edward Brown.
George Fox, *A Day-Book of Counsel and Comfort*, ed. L.V. Hodgkin. London: Macmillan and Co., 1937; p. 283.

The Ground
Julian of Norwich, *Revelations of Divine Love*, ed. Grace Warrack. London: Methuen Press; Chap. 56 (14th Rev.).
T.S. Eliot, *Complete Poems and Plays.* New York: Harcourt, Brace & World, 1952; from Chorus VII of "The Rock."

Roots
St Augustine, *An Augustine Synthesis*, ed. Erich Przywara. New York: Harper & Row, 1958; p. 339.
Harry Emerson Fosdick, *On Being Fit to Live With.* New York: Harper & Brothers, 1946; p. 55.
The Book of Common Prayer. Toronto: Anglican Book Centre, 1962; p. 128.

The Green Leaf
Thomas a Kempis, *The Imitation of Christ.* Baltimore: Penguin Books, 1952; p. 170.

Flower and Fruit
St Francis de Sales, *Introduction to the Devout Life*. London: Burns & Oates, 1956; p. 233.

The Garden
C.S. Lewis, *Letters to Malcolm*. New York: Harcourt, Brace & World, 1964; p. 19.
St Thérèse of Lisieux, *Autobiography of a Soul*, trans. Ronald Knox. London: Collins (Fontana Books), 1960; p. 26.

Fences
St Augustine, *op. cit.*, p. 369
Dietrich Bonhoeffer, *The Cost of Discipleship*, trans. R.H. Fuller. London: SCM Press, 1948; pp. 38-39.

Seedtime and Harvest
Harry Emerson Fosdick, *op. cit.*, p. 33.
Thomas Merton, *Seeds of Contemplation*. New York: Dell Publishing Co., 1960; p. 18.

Stakes and Supports
Edward Keble Talbot, *Retreat Addresses of Edward Keble Talbot*, ed. Lucy Menzies. London: SPCK, 1955; p. 47.
Saint Patrick's Breastplate, #812, *The Book of Common Praise*.

The Compost Heap
Walter Rauschenbusch, in *Inner Light (Second Series)*, ed. Edith R. Richards. London: Allen and Unwin, 1936; p. 175.

Fertilizer
Dag Hammerskjöld, *Markings*, trans. W.H. Auden and Leif Sjoberg. New York: Alfred A. Knopf, 1964; p. 83.
E. Herman, *Creative Prayer*. Cincinnati: Forward Movement Publications, p. 31.
Estelle C. Carver, *Newness of Life*, pub. by Episcopal Diocese of Western Massachusetts, 1956; p. 83.

The Gardener's Craft
Sadhu Sundar Singh, quoted in A.J. Appasamy's *The Cross Is
    Heaven*. London: Lutterworth Press, 1956; p. 49.
The Book of Common Prayer. Toronto: Anglican Book
    Centre, 1962; p. 228.

Weeds
Rackham Holt, George Washington Carver, New York:
Doubleday, Doran and Company, 1943; p. 226

Garden Pests
A Mind Awake: An Anthology of C.S. Lewis, ed. C.S. Kilby.
    New York: Harcourt, Brace & World, 1969; p. 159.
Evelyn Underhill, in *Inner Light, op. cit.*, p. 245 (quotation
    from *The School of Charity*).
John Baillie, *A Diary of Private Prayer*. London and New
    York: Oxford University Pres, 1960; p. 101.

Indoor Gardening
A. Tanqueray, *The Spiritual Life*. Tournai, Belgium: Desclee
    & Co., 1930, 2nd ed.; p. 439.
Olive Wyon, *Prayer*. Philadelphia: Fortress Press, 1960; p. 81.
Life of Lilias Trotter, *A Lectionary of Christian Prose*, ed.
    A.C. Bouquet. Derby: Peter Smith, 1965; p. 288.

The Growing Time
Hannah Whitall Smith, *The Christian's Secret of a Happy Life*.
    Westwood, N.J.: Fleming H. Revell Co., 1952; p. 183.
Nicholas Mosley, *The Life of Raymond Raynes*. London:
    Hodder & Stoughton, 1963; p. 233.

The First Frost
Antoine de St Exupéry, *The Little Prince*. New York: Har-
    court, Brace & World, 1934; Chap. 18.

The Promise of Spring
Brother Lawrence, *The Practice of the Presence of God*, ed.

Hugh Martin. London: SCM Press, 1956; p. 9.
Catherine Marshall, ed., *The Prayers of Peter Marshall*. New York: McGraw-Hill Book Company, 1949; p. 74.

The City
Madeleine L'Engle, *The Irrational Season*.
 New York: Seabury Press, 1979; p. 13
Martin Luther King, *Strength to Love*.
 London: Fontana Books, 1969, p. 95